Workbook

social & health EXPERT

Soziales & Gesundheit

von
Ephrem Wellenbrock
David Christie

Ernst Klett Verlag
Stuttgart · Leipzig

Workbook

social & health EXPERT

Soziales & Gesundheit

Autoren: Ephrem Wellenbrock, Dorsten; David Christie, Oxford

Berater: Hans-Henning Jasper, Monika Schumacher

Werkübersicht:
Schülerbuch, 978-3-12-800117-3
Lehrerhandbuch, mit Lehrer-Service-CD-ROM und 2 Audio-CDs, 978-3-12-800119-7
Workbook mit Prüfungsvorbereitung, 978-3-12-800118-0

Online-Ergänzung unter www.klett.de/online

1. Auflage 1 5 4 3 2 1 | 14 13 12 11 10

Alle Drucke dieser Auflage sind unverändert und können im Unterricht nebeneinander verwendet werden.
Die letzte Zahl bezeichnet das Jahr des Druckes.

Projektleitung: Matthias Rupp
Redaktion: Astrid Keller
Herstellung: Angelika Lindner

Gestaltung: B2 Büro für Gestaltung, Andreas Staiger, Stuttgart
Umschlaggestaltung: B2 Büro für Gestaltung, Andreas Staiger, Stuttgart
Illustrationen: Jeongsook Lee, Köln; Andreas Staiger, Stuttgart
Satz: B2 Büro für Gestaltung, Andreas Staiger
Reproduktion: Meyle + Müller Medien-Management, Pforzheim
Druck: Mediahaus Biering GmbH, München

Printed in Germany
ISBN 978-3-12-800118-0

9 783128 001180

Units and topics

Zeichenerklärung

→ SB: S. 14–15	Verweise auf das Schülerbuch
→ GS: H1, H2	Verweise auf das Grammar Summary im Schülerbuch
Video lounge	vertieftes Seh-/Hörverstehenstraining zu den BBC-Videos auf der Schüler-Medien-DVD
A 2.10	Audios und Hörtexte auf der Schüler-Medien-DVD / Audios auf den Lehrer-Audio-CDs.

1 Preparing for the world of work

1 **Write the names of the EU countries, then complete the text below.** → SB: S. 6–7

1. Ireland ______
2. ______
3. ______
4. ______
5. ______
6. ______
7. ______
8. ______
9. ______
10. ______
11. ______
12. ______
13. ______
14. ______
15. ______
16. ______
17. ______
18. ______
19. ______
20. ______
21. ______
22. ______
23. ______
24. ______
25. ______
26. ______
27. ______

Europe and the EU

The EU or European Union consists of ***(besteht aus)*** a total of **(1)** ______ countries. A small number of other countries are waiting to join. The most important of these is **(2)** ______. Three important European countries are not in the EU: Iceland, **(3)** ______ and **(4)** ______. The modern EU began in **(5)** 19______, but the first community of European countries was forty years earlier, in **(6)** ______. It was called the European Coal and Steel Community (ECSC) and its members were Germany, France, the Netherlands, Belgium, Luxembourg and Italy. The EU has many advantages for the people who live there. One is that it is much easier today than ever before to **(7)** ______ ***(reisen)*** and to **(8)** ______ ***(arbeiten)*** in another country. That means that people of different **(9)** ______ ***(Staatsangehörigkeiten)*** get to know each other better, too. A second advantage is that you can use the same money in many EU countries – the **(10)** ______. Those places where you can use this money are known as the **(11)** ______. Not all EU countries belong to this. One, of course, is **(12)** ______, where people still use the 'pound'.

2 **Henry, a Dutch student, is introducing himself at an international seminar. Find the headings below for the four speech bubbles *(Sprechblasen)*. Write in A, B, C or D.**

→ SB: S. 8–9, GS: A 1–2, A 5, A 8–12

☐ eine zeitlich begrenzte Handlung in der Gegenwart
☐ Handlungen in der Gegenwart, die auf Dauer gültig sind
☐ Zukunftspläne
☐ Ereignisse in der Vergangenheit

A Hi. My name's Henry van Etten. I live in Eindhoven in the Netherlands.

B I was born in Eindhoven and I went to school here. Last year, I started a 4-year course at an MBO, a *Middelbar Beroepsonderwijs* – you'd call that a vocational college.

C I'm training to be a nutritionist.

D One day, I hope to be self-employed as a nutritionist, but first I'm going to work for a few years with a big food producer to get experience. I'd like to travel, too, maybe to Australia or the States.

3 **Sonja Kask is another vocational student at the seminar. Complete her introduction. Use the correct tenses and forms of the verbs in brackets (. . .).**

"Hello, I'm Sonja Kask and I **(1)** come **(come)** from Estonia.
I **(2)** ________ **(live)** in the Estonian capital, Tallinn.
I **(3)** ________ **(not/be born)** there, though. When I was very small, I **(4)** ________ **(live)** in a town called Valga, in the south of Estonia. My parents **(5)** ________ **(move)** to Tallinn from Valga when I **(6)** ________ **(be)** two years old.
I **(7)** ________ **(go)** to my first school and my secondary school in Tallinn. I **(8)** ________ **(leave)** my secondary school last year and now I'm a student at a vocational college.
I **(9)** ________ **(study)** social sciences and English. It's a 30-month course and I **(10)** ________ **(enjoy)** it very much. After I finish, I **(11)** ________ **(want)** to travel. If possible, I **(12)** ________ **(go/work)** in the UK for a couple of years.
I **(13)** ________ **(visit)** London two years ago and I **(14)** ________ **(love)** the city. Then I **(15)** ________ **(plan)** to return to Estonia. I **(16)** ________ **(like)** to study to become a teacher and work at a primary school in Tallinn."

4 **Anton Stempfhuber is from Germany. Finish this text about him with the simple present or present continuous forms of the verbs. REMEMBER! Some verbs are not normally used in the present continuous.**

Anton Stempfhuber (1) _is_ (be) from Saarbrücken in western Germany. He (2) ____________ (be) 25 years old and he (3) ____________ (work) as a chef in the kitchen of one of the city's best hotels. Anton (4) ____________ (like) his job very much indeed. He (5) ____________ (have) friendly colleagues and he (6) ____________ (think) that the work is both creative and challenging. Right now, however, Anton (7) __________ (not/be) in Saarbrücken. He (8) ____________ (do) a 6-month work placement with the EU Leonardo da Vinci programme. He (9) ____________ (spend) the six months in a Michelin starred restaurant in Paris where he (10) ____________ (train) under one of France's top chefs. "The experience (11) ____________ (be) an absolute dream," says Anton. "I (12) ____________ (learn) so much here. I (13) __________ (like) Paris, too. One day, I definitely (14) ____________ (want) to work here full-time."

5 **Here's one more young European. Her name's Lucia Moreno. You meet her in your hometown in Germany and want to find out more about her. Look at Lucia's answers and complete your questions.**

You Where (1) _do you come_ from, Lucia?
Lucia I come from Segovia.
You Sorry, my geography's terrible. That's in Spain, right?
Lucia Right! It's in the centre of Spain.
You But you're in Germany right now. How long
(2) ______________________________________?
Lucia I'm spending three months here. It's part of my college course.
You Oh, you're a college student. What course
(3) ______________________________________?
Lucia I'm on a 2-year course to become a physical therapist.

You So when (4) ______________________________________?
Lucia I came here two weeks ago.

You And (5) ______________________________________?
Lucia Mmm, I don't know yet if I like the town or not. Everything is still very new and strange.

6 **Lucia has some questions for you, too. Continue your conversation with her. Write on a separate piece of paper. Begin like this:**

Lucia And what about you? Do you live here? I mean, you're German, right?

7 Match the expressions and the definitions, then use them to complete the sentences below. → SB: S. 12–13

1 o	2	3	4	5	6	7	8
9	10	11	12	13	14	15	

~~1~~	~~war~~	a	Person who buys things.
2	unthinkable	b	Countries which trade together commercially.
3	democracy	c	Rule that the government makes.
4	standard of living	d	Able to travel and move around.
5	trading bloc	e	How a country organises its schools is its ~.
6	consumer	f	If you are ~ of something you are for (not against) it.
7	right (n.)	g	If you have the ~ to do something, you are allowed to do it.
8	mobile (adj.)	h	Impossible (to imagine).
9	law	i	Political system in which people choose their politicians.
10	environment	j	The amount of money and the quality of life that people have.
11	currency	k	Second possibility.
12	alternative	l	The group of politicians who make laws for a country.
13	in favour of	m	The money that people use in a country is its ~.
14	education system	n	The world around us.
15	parliament	~~o~~	~~When two or more countries fight together.~~

1. There's a law which says that you can't smoke in restaurants.
2. Are you ______________ of the EU? – No! I'm against it.
3. What ______________ do they use in Norway? – I think it's the Krone.
4. Where does the European ______________ sit? – Well, it sits for three weeks every month in Brussels, and for one week in Strasbourg.
5. People in countries like Germany and Great Britain have a much better ______________ than people in African countries. They have more money, nicer houses, cars and so on.
6. The Second World ______________ began in 1939 and ended in 1945.
7. We don't want to do this but I'm afraid there's no ______________.
8. I'm not going to do that. It's ______________!
9. People move around more nowadays. They're much more ______________ than in the past.
10. In a ______________, people have the ______________ to choose their politicans.

8 In exercise 7 above, *four* expressions have a definition but are not in the sentences 1–10. Which? Write them here:

a ______________ b ______________ c ______________ d ______________

Now write a sentence yourself with each expression.

a ______________

b ______________

c ______________

d ______________

9 **Nationality words. Look at the table and finish the sentences below.** → SB: S.14–15

Sandra Hoffmann is from **Germany**.
She's **German**. (Or: She's **a German**.)
She loved the food that she ate in **Britain**.
She loved **British** food.
She thought **the British** were friendly.

1 -*(i)an*

Country	**Adjective**	**Person**	**Population (people)**
Germany	German	a German	the Germans
Austria	Austrian	an Austrian	the Austrians

Also: **Belgium** (Belgian / a Belgian / the Belgians); **Bulgaria** (Bulgarian / a Bulgarian / the Bulgarians); **Estonia** (Estonian); **Hungary** (Hungarian); **Italy** (Italian); **Latvia** (Latvian); **Lithuania** (Lithuanian); **Romania** (Romanian); **Slovakia** (Slovakian); **Slovenia** (Slovenian)

2 Other nationalities

Britain	British	a British person*	the British
Cyprus	Cypriot	a Cypriot	the Cypriots
Czech Republic	Czech	a Czech	the Czechs
Denmark	Danish	a Dane	the Danes
Finland	Finnish	a Finn	the Finns
France	French	a Frenchwoman/man	the French
Greece	Greek	a Greek	the Greeks
Iceland	Icelandic	an Icelander	the Icelanders
Ireland	Irish	an Irishwoman/man	the Irish
Luxembourg	Luxembourgian	a Luxembourger	the Luxembourgers
Malta	Maltese	a Maltese	the Maltese
The Netherlands	Dutch	a Dutchwoman/man	the Dutch
Norway	Norwegian	a Norwegian	the Norwegians
Poland	Polish	a Pole	the Poles
Portugal	Portuguese	a Portuguese	the Portuguese
Spain	Spanish	a Spaniard	the Spanish
Sweden	Swedish	a Swede	the Swedes
Switzerland	Swiss	a Swiss	the Swiss
Turkey	Turkish	a Turk	the Turks

** 'a Briton' is sometimes used in newspapers. In everyday language people also sometimes say: 'a Brit/the Brits'.*

1. Emma is from Finland. She's a Finn (or: She's Finnish).
2. Jan is from Poland. He's a ____________ (or: He's ____________).
3. I was in Portugal last week. ____________ food is delicious.
4. Belgium is famous for its chips. The ____________ have the best chips in Europe!
5. Norway isn't an EU country. The ____________ don't want to be part of the EU.
6. Eva is a young ____________ from Dublin in the Irish Republic.
7. The flags of Bulgaria, Italy and Hungary are all the same colour. The ____________, ____________ and ____________ flags are all red, white and green.
8. *Swatch* is a ____________ company that makes watches.
9. The movie actor Antonio Banderas is Italian, isn't he? – No! He's from Spain. He's a ____________.
10. *Glitnir* is the name of a bank in Iceland. It's the third largest ____________ bank.
11. The official currency of Turkey is the ____________ Lira (TL).

Video lounge

→ SB: S.15, Schüler DVD V1, Schüler DVD Videotext

1 **Before you watch the video, look at the vocabulary in the box and complete the sentences.**

I was supposed (to do) *ich sollte (etwas tun)*
I changed my mind *ich habe es mir anders überlegt*
be within easy reach *leicht erreichbar sein*
decamp (to) *aufbrechen (nach)*
transition *Übergang*
baggage allowance *Freigepäck(menge)*
start from scratch *bei Null anfangen*
get it together *sein Leben in den Griff bekommen*
enrol *sich anmelden*
work on (doing sth.) *dabei sein (etwas zu tun)*
Soho *Stadtteil Londons*
sign from God *Zeichen Gottes*
serve a purpose *einen Zweck erfüllen*
do some readjusting *sich neu einstellen*
pretty much *so ziemlich*
hang out (with s.o.) *(mit jmdm.) herumhängen*
there is something going on *es passiert etwas*

1. I was supposed to go to New York but I changed ________ and went to Washington DC.
2. When you fly, you are allowed to take 20kg of baggage. Your ________ is 20kg.
3. At the weekend, I often ________ my friends in town.
4. The sea is within ________ of the town and in summer everyone ________ to the beach.
5. The first thing I did when I arrived in London was to ________ at a language school.
6. They had nothing when they arrived in the new country. They had to ________ from ________.
7. However, they worked hard, made friends and slowly they got it ________.
8. There's a McDonald's in ________ every city in the world now.
9. The ________ from being a student to having a job and working isn't always easy. People often have to do some ________.
10. Have you found an apprenticeship yet? – No, but I'm ________ it!
11. Life in modern Europe is really interesting. There's ________ exciting ________.

2 **Watch the video in sections and answer the questions. Write on a separate piece of paper.**

Section 1: In the U-Bahn and at the beach.
1. Where was Seema supposed to go? Why did she change her mind and go to Berlin?
2. What things are within easy reach of Berlin city centre? What happens in summer?
3. Who spent the first weekend in Berlin with Seema? What did that give her ('Which was nice')?
4. After that weekend she was 'starting completely from scratch again'. What *three* problems does she mention? How did she feel about that situation?
5. Then she says she 'slowly got it together'. What *four* things does she mention?

Section 2: On her bike in town. Tip: Seema sometimes speaks quickly in this section. Remember that you can also read the text of the video on your DVD to help you.
6. How did Seema start learning German? Where did she find the books?
7. Enrolling at the language school in Berlin 'served two purposes' for Seema. What are the two purposes?

Section 3: In Seema's flat.
8. Why did Seema's family have 'to do some readjusting in their head' at first? How did they feel later?
9. What does she say about Europe today? What should young people do in Seema's opinion?

3 **Listen one more time and check your answers. Then write a short text about Seema – 'A Brit in Berlin'.**

More listening practice in *Social & Health Expert*
Remember that you can listen to many of the texts in your book. Look for the DVD sign: A1.1

2 Getting to know you

1 **Match the phrases on the left with those on the right and form complete sentences of a dialogue.**

→ SB: S.18–19

1 And how then did …
2 So are you …
3 I'm here on a trainee …
4 I am training to become a dietician and work for …
5 ~~Do you mind …~~
6 Pleased to meet you Jane, …
7 By the way, …
8 I see. Which job do you …
9 Yes, I do. The food is nice, …
10 Goldbrecht and the Norwich based company Nourwell Ltd …
11 No, actually I'm German. I'm …
12 So what are you doing …
13 No, not at all, …
14 Where do you come from? Are …
15 Exactly, we have more or …
16 I see. That means that someone from …
17 Is this your first …
18 No, I was in London with my parents …
19 What about you? Have …
20 No, I have to admit that …

a the people are friendly and I like the music.
b ~~if I join you?~~
c from Braunschweig, that's in Lower Saxony.
d take a seat.
e are business partners. They have agreed on a mutual trainee programme.
f here in Norwich, Gerrit?
g the German food producer Goldbrecht. They mainly make convenience food such as pizza, lasagne etc.
h programme for six months.
i you end up here in Norwich?
j my name's Gerrit, Gerrit Mühlkamp.
k you Swedish?
l do and which company do you work for?
m enjoying the party so far?
n I'm Jane, Jane Wilkins.
o Norwich is now staying in Braunschweig with your company?
p less swapped our workplaces for half a year.
q when I was 10 or 11. But I have to admit that I do not remember that much.
r visit to the UK?
s I haven't. But I spent a week in Zurich two years ago.
t you ever been to Germany?

1		2		3		4		5	b	6		7		8	
9		10		11		12		13		14		15		16	
17		18		19		20									

2 **Now decide who says what and arrange the sentences in a logical order so that you get a conversation between the two people. Of course you can continue the conversation if you want to.**

Jane Wilkins	**Gerrit Mühlkamp**
______________________	______________________
______________________	______________________
______________________	______________________
______________________	______________________
______________________	______________________
______________________	______________________
______________________	______________________
______________________	______________________
______________________	______________________

3 Have a look at the following word webs. They deal with topics that might come up in a conversation. Find as many words and expressions as possible that have to do with the topic given. One word web has already been done for you.

LIKES AND DISLIKES OF YOUR JOB

- not enough time for the patients
- not too much routine
- responsibility
- night shifts
- getting up early
- the pay
- challenging situations
- a lot of people to talk to
- having to work weekends
- overtime

1.

TALKING ABOUT YOUR HOBBIES AND INTERESTS

2.

WHERE YOU LIVE

3.

FUTURE PLANS

4 **Have a look at the following situations and act out dialogues with a partner. Be as creative and realistic as possible.**

→ SB: S. 22–23

1. It's your first day in a retirement home in London. You meet an elderly lady in front of the reception …
2. It's the first day of your work placement in Harrogate. You enter your office where you see the company's personnel manager and a lady you have never seen before …
3. It's your friend's birthday party in Berlin. You sit next to someone at the table who obviously does not speak any German at all …
4. Your hospital is organising a conference on pain management. One of the speakers is a renowned doctor from Washington, D.C. It is your job to look after him during the day. In the reception area you see a man who seems to be waiting for someone …

3 Working with children

1 **Find the odd one out. In each line there is one word that does not fit. Find the word and explain in one sentence why this word does not belong here. Sometimes there is more than one correct answer.**

→ SB: S. 24–25

driver – teacher – parents rep – headmaster
Headmaster does not fit because all the other people do not do most of their work in an office.

1. driver – teacher – pupil – parent
2. parents rep – pupil – headmistress – driver
3. janitor – parent – driver – music teacher
4. teaching assistant – teacher – special needs teacher – nurse
5. deputy – headmistress – parents rep – driver
6. to learn – to teach – to support – to oversee
7. lesson – break – afternoon – assembly
8. administration – timetabling – telephoning – teaching
9. office – classroom – conference room – bus

2 **Talking about your job. Match the quotations on the right with the corresponding job title on the left.**

1 ~~nurse~~
2 parents rep
3 driver
4 deputy
5 secretary
6 headmistress
7 special needs teacher
8 janitor
9 teaching assistant

a "I am responsible for most of the paperwork."
b "Timetabling is one of my favourite responsibilities."
c ~~"Fortunately we do not get many accidents. There are only minor injuries I have to look after."~~
d "Sometimes I am just sad that I spend most of my time in an office and not in a classroom with the pupils."
e "I try to represent the parents and their concerns."
f "Especially in the mornings when I pick up all the pupils they can be extremely noisy."
g "Teaching is much more demanding than I thought!"
h "The pupils with disabilities should be taught together with the other pupils. Sometimes they just need a bit more help."
i "I am glad that sometimes parents help me when I have to replace or repair things in the school."

1	2	3	4	5	6	7	8	9
c								

3 Organising a school exchange. The flow chart below shows you important steps in setting up a school exchange. Fill in the missing information.

→ SB: S. 28 – 29

idea: let's organise a school exchange

↓

1. ______________________________

↓

2. get to know your partner school

↓

3. ______________________________

↓

4. agree on a programme

↓

5. ______________________________

↓

6. make necessary travel arrangements

↓

7. ______________________________

↓

8. ______________________________

↓

9. plan for next year's exchange

4 Have a look at the following sentences describing St. Anne's Primary School in Eastbourne. Arrange the sentences in an order that makes sense to you.

a Fortunately, this is one of Mrs Hodges main responsibilities. She is St. Anne's deputy.
b 16 female and 7 male members of staff work here.
c This year, there are 634 pupils attending St. Anne's Primary School.
d ~~Founded in 1902, St. Anne's Primary School is one of the oldest primary schools in Eastbourne.~~
e The school has its own gym and a new assembly hall.
f There are about 37 pupils who get extra support by special needs teachers.
g The school's new headmistress, Jane Stuart, started her job last year.
h She likes talking to teachers and parents but dislikes timetabling.

1	d	2		3		4		5		6		7		8	

5 **Now continue to describe St. Anne's Primary School using the following notes. Write complete sentences.**

a last year exchange programme with German school in Cologne
b 2009: award healthy school meal
c playground and playing field next to gym
d very efficient cooperation with parents

1. ______________________________

2. ______________________________

3. ______________________________

4. ______________________________

6 **Now include your sentences into the description of St. Anne's Primary School and write down the sentences.**

1. ______________________________

2. ______________________________

3. ______________________________

4. ______________________________

5. ______________________________

6. ______________________________

7. ______________________________

8. ______________________________

9. ______________________________

10. ______________________________

11. ______________________________

12. ______________________________

Video lounge

→ SB: S. 33, Schüler DVD V2, Schüler DVD Videotext

1 **Before you watch the video, complete the following sentences so that they express your opinion about the schooling topics mentioned. Of course you may write more than just one sentence each!**

1. In traditional schools most of the decisions are made ____________________
2. Parents, the government and the teachers ____________________
3. The topics and the subjects the pupils have to study ____________________
4. Rules are ____________________
5. Lessons normally ____________________
6. For the pupils, taking classes is ____________________
7. Many experts discuss the best ways to learn. I believe ____________________

2 **Watch the video in sections. While watching note all the information about the following topics. Write on a separate piece of paper. The vocabulary in the box can help you.**

Vocabulary

to turn sth. on its head *etwas auf den Kopf stellen*
to take a class *eine Klasse besuchen*
to be forced to *müssen*
to zero in on sth. *sich auf etwas konzentrieren*
to go after sth. *sich um etwas bemühen*
might *Macht*
since ancient times *seit alters her*
to put down *abwehren, demütigen*
to have equal rights *gleichberechtigt sein*
to judge *beurteilen*
vote *Stimme*
to bother *sich bemühen*
to hire *einstellen*
to fire *entlassen*
election *Wahl*
to make the grade *den Anforderungen gerecht werden*
ability *Fähigkeit*
to fit in *sich einfügen*

Topics on Sudbury Valley School:

- general information
- experiment
- difference
- taking classes
- lessons
- what to learn
- how to learn
- rules
- decisions
- teachers

3 **Write a short text using the ideas you started with in exercise 1. Compare a traditional school with Sudbury Valley School in the USA.**

4 Writing emails

1 **Write the email addresses.**

→ SB: S. 38–39

1. Mike dot Harris at Google dot com — mike.harris@google.com
2. L dot Williams at BT hyphen Online dot [ko] dot U-K ______
3. Ina dot Krüger at Web dot D-E ______
4. Liv dot Wagner at Markert underscore sales dot D-E ______
5. Bodo hyphen Richter at Köln underscore net dot D-E ______

2 **Be polite. Look at the examples, then write the sentences below again with *would* or *could*.**

***Would / Could you* + noun**		
Would you (please) Could you (please)	send me email me let me have	your monthly failure rates for March? the dates of the next meeting? the address of a good hotel?

***Would / Could you* + *when / where / if* (= ob)**			
Would you (please) Could you (please)	tell me let me know	when where if	you will be in Germany? the meeting will be? Mr Smith is in the office today?

1. Send me the dates of the health fair next month.
   Would you please send me the dates of the health fair next month?
2. Email me the name of your new assistant.
   ______
3. Let me have the telephone number of your Irish office.
   ______
4. When will you send your report *(Bericht)*?
   Could you tell me / let me know when you will send your report?
5. Where are your distribution offices in the Netherlands?
   ______
6. Do you have Ms Jones's mobile number?
   ______
7. Email me the dates when your office will be closed.
   ______
8. Will someone meet me at the airport?
   ______
9. Where is the new dental laboratory?
   ______
10. Let us have your decision asap.
    ______

3 **Read the emails and answer the questions below in English. You can use notes.**

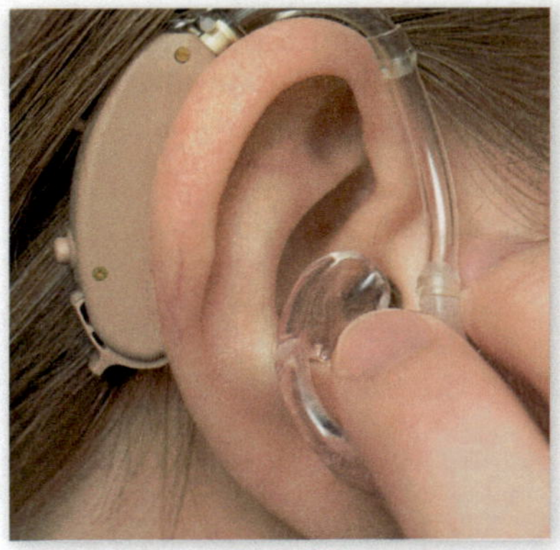

SITUATION
You work as an apprentice for the German company Audiwell, a producer of hearing devices *(Hörgeräte)*. Audiwell has sales offices throughout Europe and the USA. The various hearing aids are produced in the company's manufacturing facility in Ulm. During your apprenticeship you are also working in the sales department. Your boss there is Ann-Katrin Dabbert. This morning, you have these emails in your inbox *(Posteingang)*.

Von: rafael.costa@audiwell.es
Gesendet: 24. Oktober 20 _ _ 15:29
An: your name@audiwell.de
Betreff: AW: health fair in Madrid
Anhang: Health_Fair.doc (105 KB)

Dear *(Your name)*
Thanks for your email. You asked about the health fair in Madrid next month.
In the attachment you'll find full details of dates etc. Please let me know if I can help further.
Kind regards
Rafael

Von: melissa.taylor@audiwell.co.uk
Gesendet: 24. Oktober 20 _ _ 17.15
An: your name@audiwell.de
Betreff: product launch

Dear *(Your name)*
We're all very excited here in the London office about the launch in January of the new hearing device AW75+. Could you let us have any sales literature asap so that we can translate it into English? Thanks in advance!
All the best
Melissa

Von: melissa.taylor@audiwell.co.uk
Gesendet: 24. Oktober 20 _ _ 17.18
An: your name@audiwell.de
Betreff: Ms Dabbert's next visit

Dear *(Your name)*
Me again! Sorry, I forgot to ask something in my last email. Could you also send us the dates of Ms Dabbert's next visit to the UK and let me know if you would like me to arrange hotels, a hire car etc.?

All the best
Melissa

Von: wim.de_vries@audiwell.nl
Gesendet: 24. Oktober 20 _ _ 18.04
An: your name@audiwell.de
Betreff: office reorganisation

Hi *(Your name)*
Hope all's well with you in Germany. This is to let you know that the Amsterdam office will be closed for two days next month (28 and 29 November) while we reorganise and install a new computer network. Sounds great fun ☹
Best wishes
Wim de Vries

► **product launch** *Produkteinführung* ► **sales literature** *Verkaufsprospekte* ► **hire car** *Mietwagen*

1. Who is asking you for information, documents etc.? What do they want?

____

____

2. Who is giving you information? What is the information?

____

____

4 You talk to your boss, Frau Dabbert, and make notes about how to reply to the four emails. Write the emails. Use your dictionary if necessary. The first one is partly done for you.

→ SB: S. 40 – 41

Rafael
- Danke für die Infos über die Messe.
- Bitte senden Sie uns eine Liste von guten Hotels in Madrid. Danke im Voraus!

Melissa (E-Mail 1)
- Danke für die E-Mail. Wir freuen uns auch über die Produkteinführung. Verkaufsprospekte werden am 15. November erhältlich sein. Wir werden sie sofort per Post versenden (we'll send).

Melissa (E-Mail 2)
- In der Anlage finden Sie die Details zu Frau Dabberts nächstem Besuch.
- Hotels können wir hier buchen, aber bitte einen Mietwagen vom 4.-8. Dez. besorgen. Danke!

Wim
- Danke für die Infos.
- Bitte sagen Sie uns Bescheid, ob wir Sie am 28. und 29. Nov. per Telefon erreichen können. Haben Sie auch eine Mobilnummer?
- Bitte schicken Sie uns bis (by) 27. Nov. Ihre monatlichen Ausfallraten für November.
- Viel Glück beim Umzug!

An: rafael.costa@audiwell.es
Kopie an: a-k.dabbert@audiwell.de
Betreff: AW: AW: health fair in Madrid

Dear Rafael

Thanks very much for the information about **(1)** ______________________ You asked very kindly if you could help further. Yes please! **(2)** ______________________ us a list of good hotels in Madrid? Thanks **(3)** ________!

Best regards

(Your name)

5 Each email phrase has a missing word. What is it?

1. Thanks ___in___ advance!
2. In the ____________ you'll find …
3. Could you please ____________ me know …
4. Looking ____________ to hearing from you soon.
5. You ____________ to know …
6. You ____________ about …
7. Please let me know if you have any ____________ questions.
8. I'm ____________ I haven't replied before.
9. I'm ____________ I don't have the information you asked about.
10. I'm sorry you couldn't ____________ the file.
11. How are ____________ going?
12. ____________, thanks.
13. I'm ____________ the document you asked for.
14. ____________ you please tell me … ?

5 Working with the elderly

1 **Complete the crossword puzzle. Terms that consist of two words should be spelled with a blank *(Leerzeichen)*.**

→ SB: S. 42–43

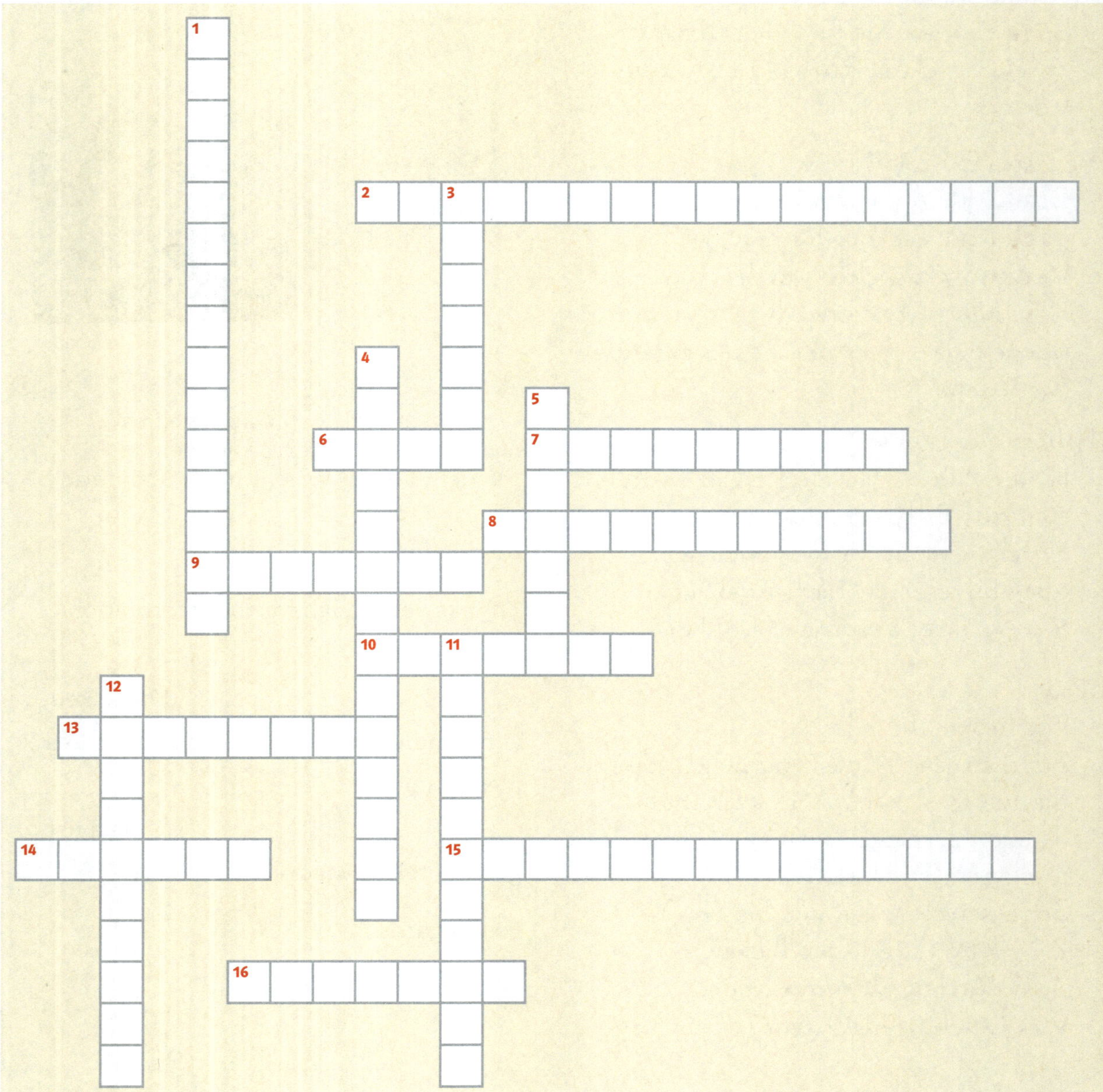

ACROSS

2 someone who assists individuals with healthcare needs
6 special attention focussing on health and hygiene
7 medicine that is injected into the skin
8 working when other people sleep
9 what somebody leaves on the answerphone
10 people who are old
13 someone who lives in a retirement home
14 health expert
15 paperwork
16 someone who cleans and maintains a building

DOWN

1 house where mostly elderly people who need some kind of assistance live
3 everyday jobs
4 referring to drugs and medicines
5 someone who comes around to say hello
11 something that makes a room more attractive, e.g. for a party
12 medicine

2 **Before you read the text, look at the following common fears and worries that people associate with getting older. What would your answer be?**

→ SB: S. 46 – 47

Example: "I am afraid of depending on others."
Possible answer: "I can understand that this worries you but there is nothing wrong with accepting help. Accepting help means that you remain flexible."

Here are other fears and worries:
- living in a nursing home
- running out of money
- being lonely

3 **Now read the following text and complete the word web on the next page with information from the text.**

Getting older

Many people are afraid of what may happen as they get older. Some worry about their health, others fear they might lose their independence. Here's a list of the most common fears and worries:

- losing one's energy and optimism
- running out of money
- not being able to concentrate anymore
- not being flexible anymore
- living in a nursing home
- needing a wheelchair
- depending on others
- being ill very often
- suffering from pain
- suffering from the side effects of medication
- being lonely

Despite these common fears health experts and psychologists say that it is important to accept that we are getting older. They suggest actively fighting the problems that might come up when you grow older. The most decisive step is not to get stressed just because you are getting older. Getting older is part of our lives and cannot be ignored or prevented. The only thing you can influence is how you feel when you get older.

Doctors and other health experts advise their patients to get enough exercise and eat healthy food. You do not need a gym for your exercise, just take regular walks around your neighbourhood or the local park. This is also a good way to meet people who live near you. The sooner you make regular physical exercise a part of your daily routine the better for you and your personal fitness.

Make sure to see your doctor regularly. Do not wait too long with these appointments. There are some illnesses that can be prevented or cured if you get an early diagnosis. Ask your doctor to explain any possible side effects of your medication. If you suffer from an illness, try to learn as much as possible about it.

Keeping one's mind active is of key importance. Do crossword puzzles or other puzzles to keep your mind sharp. Play chess or some other game that requires a lot of thinking. Read books that trigger your imagination.

Make sure that there are enough people around you can talk to. Socialising is a very good way to stop yourself from worrying too much. Develop a network of friends and get involved in different social groups. Friends can reduce loneliness and also make us feel better. Use the internet to keep in contact with friends who live far away. Do your own research about the things that interest you.

GETTING OLDER: WHAT TO DO NOT TO WORRY ABOUT IT

social contacts	mental fitness

physical fitness and nutrition	medical issues	your attitude

4 Add your own ideas and tips to complete the word web.

5 Now prepare a three-minute talk in which you give advice on how to deal with people who express a fear of getting old.

6 Complete the following table.
Example: to inject – injection

→ SB: S. 52 (word families)

	VERB	NOUN
1	to care	
2		retirement
3	to decorate	
4		arrangement
5	to deliver	
6	to chat	
7		arrival
8		signature
9	to repair	
10		access
11		requirements
12	to decide	
13		plan
14	to choose	
15		assistance
16	to transport	
17	to lift	
18		visit
19	to promise	

7 Now make sentences on *Working with the elderly* using as many of the words above as possible.

6 Being sensitive

1 **Complete the sentences with words from the box.**

→ SB: S. 54–55

challenges • ~~bereavement~~ • staff • detached • professional • member • pain • grief • strongly • condolence • death • behaviour • patients • affected • cope • emotions • loss

After the lecture given by a visiting professor at their hospital Pam and Nadia discuss what they have just heard. The professor talked about how to deal with (1) bereavement and grieving (2) ________ in a professional way.

This is something that doctors, nurses and other medical staff need to be able to (3) ________ with. Especially in situations that involve the (4) ________ of a relative or a close friend.

(5) ________ is a strong feeling that family members may want to express to help them deal with the (6) ________ of someone they love.

Of course, for medical staff the (7) ________ way of dealing with these situations is to feel (8) ________ from any individual fate – but of course there might be patients you liked a lot and it touches you deeply when they die.

Sometimes you might feel that you want to express how (9) ________ you feel to somebody but you are not sure if the person will be able to talk. Here it might be a good idea to send a (10) ________ letter if you feel very close to the patient's family. But of course a condolence letter is a letter you send as a private individual, not as a (11) ________ of the hospital staff.

No matter how much you are (12) ________ by death, loss and (13) ________ it is part of your professional (14) ________ to deal with these situations in such a way that you are not governed by your (15) ________.

Student nurses Pam and Nadia regard dealing with death as one of the major (16) ________ of their job. Of course, they are sure that they will get more and more experience, but they also believe that medical (17) ________ sometimes need professional help to cope with extreme situations as well.

2 **Find synonyms in the text (exercise 1) for the following expressions.**

1. to manage something ________
2. to mourn ________
3. bereavement ________
4. to be saddened ________
5. family member ________
6. to express one's condolences ________
7. sympathy ________

3 **Study the following diagram about active listening. Add any aspects to the diagram you consider important. Prepare a three-minute talk on active listening which you then give to the class.**

→ SB: S. 58 – 59

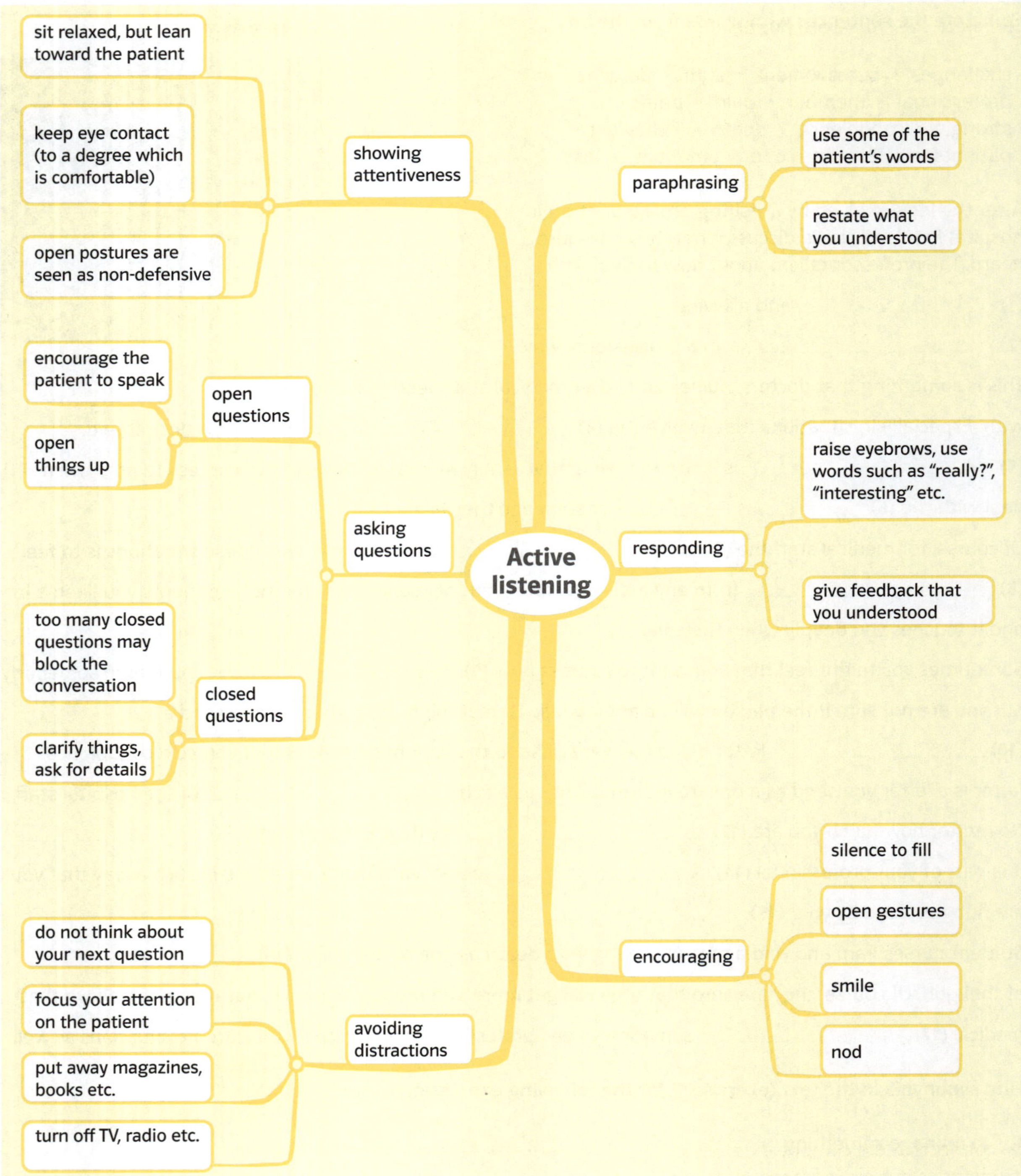

Structure for your talk:

1. ______________________________

2. ______________________________

3. ______________________________

4. ______________________________

...

7 Working with addiction

1 Complete the crossword puzzle. → SB: S. 60–61

ACROSS

1 causing harm
3 something causing problems
6 to limit
10 injury, damage
11 connected to a computer network
14 changes in function, sensation or appearance indicating a disease or disorder
15 something that cannot be stopped
16 to forbid
19 someone who is addicted
21 an activity that is diverting
22 to pay out, to give away
23 something required
24 leaves of a certain plant dried and prepared for smoking

DOWN

2 obsession, compulsion
4 an act which is against the law
5 brutal force
7 medical care provided to improve a person's state
8 beliefs and norms of a person
9 playing for stakes (often money) in the hope of winning
12 inhalation of smoke from tobacco products used by others
13 short for television
17 be fully aware of something
18 worldwide network of computers
20 to rest, to become less tense

2 **Study the word web about alcohol addiction. Then make sentences using as many of the words from the word web as possible. Write on a separate piece of paper.**

Many teenagers drink far too much at weekends and come home drunk. They go out to pubs and bars with their friends.

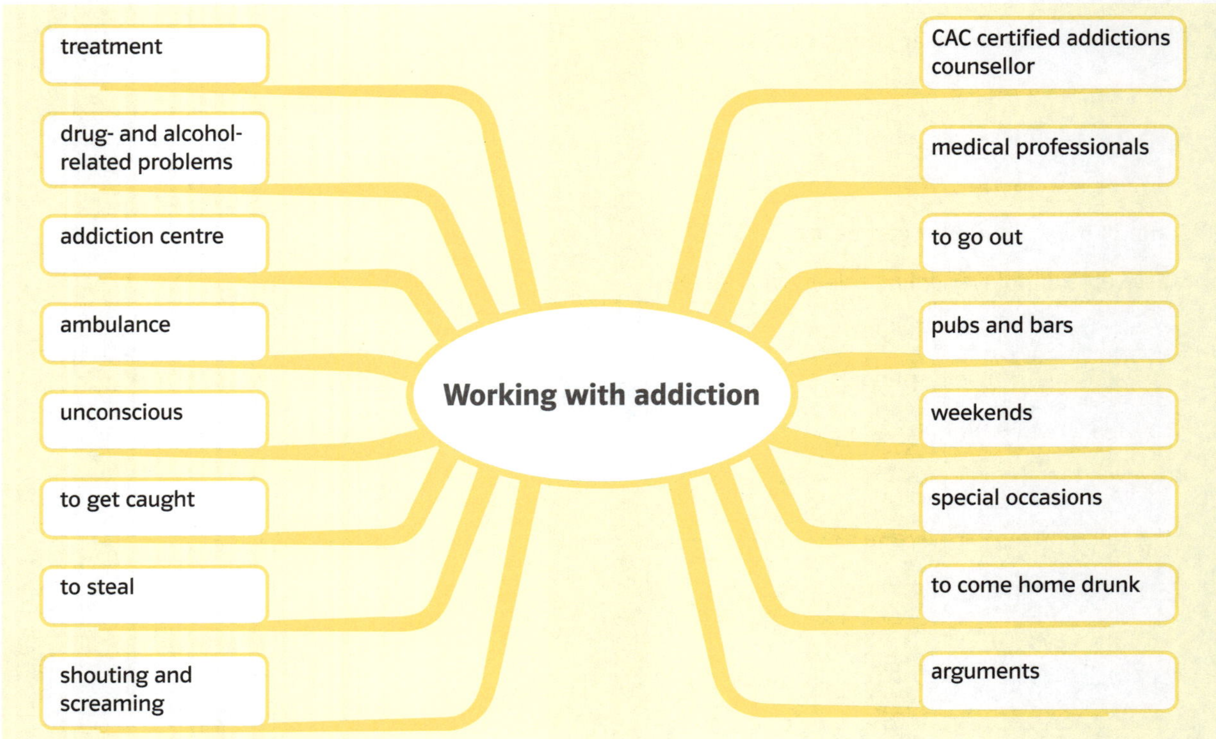

3 **Complete the sentences with the correct form of the word – adjective or adverb. In the grid on the right, tick (✓) the boxes for which sort of word you have used. Finish the exercise before checking the answers.**

→ SB: S. 62–63, GS: F1–3

	ADJ.	ADV.
1. large: I work for a large company in Germany.	✓	
2. famous: The company is ______ for its electronic products.		
3. easy: You can buy many things very ______ online today.		
4. quick: When you order things online they usually arrive ______ .		
5. interesting: I read this ______ book last week about marketing.		
6. amazing: The author had some ______ ideas.		
7. excellent: This is an ______ new product.		
8. interested: I think people will be very ______ in it.		
9. careful: Be ______ when you cross the street in England.		
10. careful: Always cross the street ______ in England.		
11. automatic: This is an ______ door.		
12. automatic: It opens ______ when you're near it.		
13. extreme: The company's customer service department is ______ good.		
14. amazing: They're ______ efficient.		
15. total: Lots of people think George is ______ crazy.		
16. incredible: In fact, he's ______ clever.		

4 **First complete the following sentences about computer games. Then arrange them in a logical order and add further sentences writing a short article on computer games.**

→ SB: S. 64–65

a Many experts believe that online computer games are ______ ☐
b Despite these games' international success they warn ______ ☐
c Some of the most popular games have more than ______ ☐
d These games are ______ ☐
e Even though the players say ______ ☐
f World of Warcraft is ______ ☐
g Some of these computer games are classified as ______ ☐
h Massively multiplayer online role-playing games ______ ☐
i Many computer games include several common themes ______ ☐
j Today, millions of users spend ______ 1
k Parents complain that ______ ☐
l However, teenagers defend themselves and ______ ☐

5 **Find the odd one out. Prepare to give reasons for your decisions.**

→ SB: S. 66–69

1. toxic – poisonous – dangerous – bad
______
2. alcohol – tobacco – marijuana – TV
______
3. gambling – smoking – drinking – stealing
______
4. therapy – treatment – programme – help
______
5. resident – patient – addict – handicapped
______
6. meditation – concentration – fulfilment – breathing exercise
______
7. drinker – addict – AA member – patient
______
8. foreign – anonymous – not known – unknown
______
9. reluctant – unwilling – hesitant – refusing
______
10. prohibited – illegal – forbidden – criminal
______
11. anxiety – fear – nervousness – restlessness
______

6 **Work with a partner. Use the vocabulary of unit 7 and make your own list of words including one odd one out. Now show your list to your partner and ask him/her to find the odd one out.**

Video lounge

→ SB: S. 69, Schüler DVD V3, Schüler DVD Videotext

1 **Before you watch the video, have a close look at the following statements and the vocabulary in the box.**

Vocabulary

to thrive *florieren, gedeihen*
binge drinking *Komasaufen*
to down *hinunterschütten, in sich hineinschütten*
intoxication *Rausch, Trunkenheit*
long-term damage *Langzeitschäden*
alcohol-related *alkoholbedingt*
revenue *Einkünfte, Einnahmen*
to tie up *blockieren*
council *Gemeinderat*
to offset *gegenrechnen*
approach *Ansatz, Herangehensweise*
shift *Verlagerung, Verschiebung*
to have a night out *(abends) ausgehen*
moderating *mäßigend*
to achieve *erreichen*

a ☐ There is an increasing culture of intoxication.

b ☐ The government wants a shift to continental café-style drinking.

c ☐ If older people came into the city centres, that could be a moderating influence on young people's behaviour.

d ☐ Binge drinking has been defined as consuming more than four pints or a bottle of wine in one session.

e ☐ Nearly half of all men and a quarter of all women have become binge drinkers.

f ☐ Binge drinking is doing long-term damage to our society.

g ☐ The biggest increase is among 18- to 24-year olds.

Now watch the video and number the statements in the order in which they appear.

2 **Watch the video again and note down further aspects which are important.**

____

____

____

____

____

____

____

____

____

____

____

3 **Now write a short German summary of the video using your notes.**

8 Talking about your workplace

1 Match the phrases on the left with those on the right to form complete sentences.

→ SB: S.72–73

1	~~People in the same profession …~~	a	on company premises where the staff can have their lunch.
2	The term *workforce* is used to describe …	b	you are at work is the shift.
3	The money which is given …	c	during one's working hours in which an employee is allowed to take time off from the job.
4	Any work which is done in addition to …	d	that an employee spends at paid work.
5	A certain and specialized division of an organisation or a company …	e	are done in an office.
6	Many business activities …	f	i.e. the building in which you work.
7	The time in which …	g	by the employer in return for work is the pay.
8	A canteen is a restaurant …	h	is a person who exercises control and makes decisions.
9	A break at work is a period of time …	i	is called a department.
10	Working time is the period of time …	j	~~are called colleagues.~~
11	The workplace includes the physical work site …	k	all the staff working for a single company or an organisation.
12	In a workplace context a boss …	l	the regular working hours stipulated in the contract is called overtime.

1	2	3	4	5	6	7	8
9	10	11	12				

2 Complete the text with words from the box.

respect • colleagues • performance • co-workers • attitude • co-operation • criticism • spend • gossip • relationship • object • makes • extra-work • waste • atmosphere • competitors • useful

As most people **(1)** ____________ more than half a day at work it might be a good idea to see their **(2)** ____________ and themselves as a team and behave like members of a big family. Of course, you don't have to be friends with all your **(3)** ____________, but you do need to be friendly.
Above all, you need your colleagues' goodwill and **(4)** ____________ if you want to get your own job done. Studies have found that arguments with colleagues and a bad (5) ____________ at work deflate morals and have a bad influence on your work **(6)** ____________.
It is important to remember that even at work we are all people and have to **(7)** ____________ each other; we should be polite and try to help each other as often as necessary. We should have a positive **(8)** ____________ at work, should try to avoid **(9)** ____________ for our colleagues or in case we have something to **(10)** ____________ we should treat the situation with diplomacy and decency. So what is it that **(11)** ____________ a good colleague?

A good colleague

- will listen to their fellow workers and will offer **(12)** ____________ advice where necessary,
- will not spread **(13)** ____________ when trusted with confidential information,
- will try and make the **(14)** ____________ at their place of work as happy and fun as possible,
- will not **(15)** ____________ their colleagues' time,
- will join some **(16)** ____________ activities such as the company's sports group etc.,
- will not see fellow workers as **(17)** ____________.

3 **Summarise the following German blog entry in English.**

So sieht mein idealer Arbeitsplatz aus:

Das Klima und die Atmosphäre im gesamten Unternehmen sind freundschaftlich und locker. Natürlich respektiert man sich, es wird aber z.B. nicht einfach geduzt. Wenn man Fragen hat, wird man unterstützt, auch wenn die Beantwortung der Fragen die Kollegen etwas mehr Zeit kostet.

Einstellungen und Beförderungen erfolgen strikt nach Befähigung und Leistung, Beziehungen etc. spielen keine Rolle. An meinem idealen Arbeitsplatz gibt es viele Angestellte mit Behinderungen. Sie werden aber nicht als Behinderte gesehen, die das Unternehmen Geld kosten, sondern sind wertvolle Mitarbeiter, die über eigene Qualifikationen und Ideen verfügen.

An meinem idealen Arbeitsplatz gibt es eine Kantine, das Essen ist gut und umsonst. Es gibt keine vorgeschriebenen Arbeits- und Anwesenheitszeiten. Wenn man seine Arbeit erledigt hat, kann man nach Hause gehen. Genauso ist es egal, ob man im Büro oder von zu Hause aus arbeitet.

Die Bezahlung ist gut, man hat nicht das Gefühl, zu wenig für seinen Einsatz zurück zu bekommen. Außerdem gibt es die Chance auf Beförderung, wenn man mehr erreichen möchte. Man muss nicht um Urlaubstermine streiten. Die Vorgesetzten wissen, wovon sie reden, sie können beurteilen, wer gute Arbeit leistet, und sind fair und wertschätzend in ihrer Rückmeldung.

4 **Now exchange ideas about your ideal workplace with your partner. Here are some criteria you might want to include, of course you can add further aspects.**

atmosphere
working hours
pay
holidays
boss/superiors
colleagues
...

9 Violence and crime

1 Arrange the words in categories of your choice. Add more words to complete your categories. Talk with a partner about your categories and your vocabulary.

→ SB: S.78–79

theft · sexual abuse · violence · domestic violence · mugging · murder · crime victim · robbery · rape · school violence · kidnapping · to rob · software piracy · drug dealer · law · gun violence · assault · organised crime · burglar · to destroy · abuse · to attack · justice · criminal record · burglary · to murder · manslaughter · vandal · drug abuse · damage to property · to rape · to steal · killer · vandalism · to break into · fraud · crime prevention · to insult someone

Category:	**Category:**
Category:	**Category:**

2 **Summarise the main results of this table about crime in Germany in a short English text.**

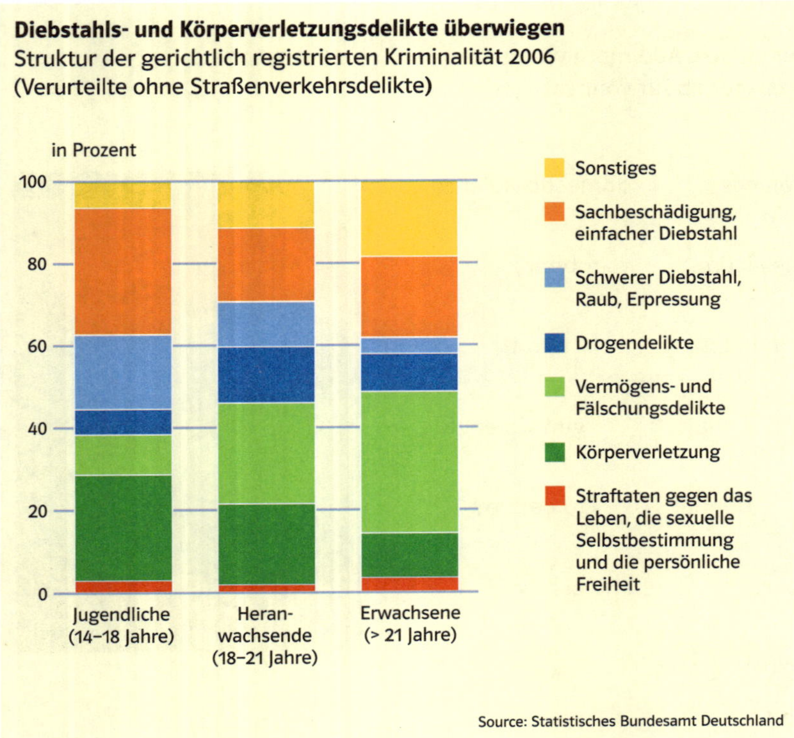

3 **Do we need crime statistics? Summarise the following statements against crime statistics in short English sentences.**

1. Kriminalität kann nicht gemessen werden.
2. In den Statistiken zur Kriminalität findet man nur das, womit sich Polizei und Justiz auseinander setzen.
3. Eine Statistik kann nicht die Zahl der tatsächlichen Gesetzesverletzungen abbilden.
4. Polizei und Staatsanwaltschaft können in vielen Bereichen nur tätig werden, wenn eine Anzeige erstattet wurde.
5. Wenn es laut Statistik in Deutschland mehr Körperverletzungen gibt, liegt das auch daran, dass sich viele Geschädigte heute eher als früher trauen, zur Polizei zu gehen.
6. Nicht nur die Zahlen in den Statistiken ändern sich, sondern auch die Gesellschaft, in der Kriminalität begangen wird. Dies wird in bloßen Zahlen nicht erfasst.
7. Internationale Statistiken erfassen nicht, wenn in unterschiedlichen Ländern unterschiedliches Verhalten als kriminell bezeichnet wird. Wenn etwa der Konsum von Cannabis in einigen Ländern verboten, woanders aber erlaubt ist, können in diesem Bereich keine Vergleiche angestellt werden.

4 **Now add arguments which speak in favour of crime statistics. Of course, you can add further arguments against crime statistics as well.**

5 **Have a look at the following list of criminal activities. For each crime, say how dramatic you judge the legal offence. Is it a petty crime, a criminal offence or a major crime? What should the punishment be? Give reasons. The first one has been done for you.**

petty crime: warning, minor punishment such as a fee
criminal offence: fine, suspension of sentence on probation
major crime: drastic punishment, such as imprisonment

CRIME	YOUR OPINION
drunk driving	This clearly is a major crime and should receive drastic punishment because those who drink and drive put others in danger as well. This is an absolutely irresponsible behaviour.
tax evasion *(Steuerhinterziehung)*	
regularly smoking cannabis	
fare dodging *(Schwarzfahren)*	
cruelty against animals	
throwing litter out of cars	
shop lifting *(Ladendiebstahl)*	
blackmailing *(Erpressung)*	
driving without a licence	
illegal music downloads	
software piracy	

Video lounge

→ SB: S. 87, Schüler DVD V4, Schüler DVD Videotext

1 Watch the video about CCTV in Britain and complete the following diagram. Watch the video as often as necessary to get all the relevant information and have a look at the vocabulary.

Vocabulary

closed-circuit television (CCTV) *Videoüberwachung*
to alert *alarmieren*
to give chase to somebody *jdn. verfolgen*
to abandon *fallen lassen*
to make off *sich davonmachen*
vehicle *Fahrzeug*
badge *Plakette*
bumper *Stoßstange*
home office *Innenministerium*
to reassure *beruhigen*
reduction in crime *Rückgang der Kriminalität*
convicted *überführt, verurteilt*
surveillance camera *Überwachungskamera*
to persuade *überzeugen*
to go straight *sauber bleiben*
to make a run for it *weglaufen*
infringement of civil liberties *Verstoß gegen die Bürgerrechte*

CCTV

arguments against CCTV	views of the general public

efficiency of CCTV	reasons for installing CCTV	how it works

2 Do you think CCTV cameras should be introduced in German city centres as well? Collect arguments for and against.

For CCTV	Against CCTV

3 Now write a comment on CCTV systems in German city centres.

10 Handling the telephone

1 **Match the situations on the left with the suitable reactions on the right.** → SB: S. 90–91
Some of the reactions can be used several times.

1 You urgently need to speak to somebody who is not available at the moment.
2 The person you want to talk to is not available.
3 Nobody answers the phone.
4 You do not understand the person at the other end of the line.
5 The caller wants to speak to your boss who is not in.
6 The caller did not understand your name.
7 You do not know who the caller is.
8 The caller urgently wants to speak to your boss who is not in.
9 Before you finish the call you want to check that everything is okay.
10 The line is busy.
11 You have got the wrong number.
12 The person you want to talk to seems to be unknown in the organisation you are calling.

a You repeat your name and offer to spell it.
b You ask for the caller's name and the company.
c You repeat the message the caller leaves.
d You check again if you have got the right number.
e You ask the caller to leave a message.
f You offer to give him your boss's mobile number.
g You ask for the person's mobile number.
h You ask him/her to repeat his/her name.
i You phone directory enquiries.
j You leave a message.
k You call again later.
l You leave a message on the answerphone.

1	2	3	4	5	6	7	8
g							

9	10	11	12

2 **Write down what you would say in the situations from exercise 1.**

3 **A message on the answerphone. Complete the sentences below with a suitable word or phrase.**

(1) This is ______ Brian Everthorpe from Bluecreek Laboratories in Manchester. This is a (2) ______ for Dr Jürgen Stein. Mr Stein, thank you very much for the blood samples which we (3) ______ yesterday. I'm glad that your hospital has decided to take part in this (4) ______ and we are really looking forward (5) ______ the results from Germany. In order to give you a more detailed account of the holistic (6) ______ we are developing with the Manchester Institute of Drug Treatment I would like to (7) ______ you to a conference taking place in Dover next month from the 17th to the 19th. Hopefully all of the European partners will find the time to come to the UK so that we can discuss (8) ______ of our project.
Of course, I will send you a formal invitation by (9) ______ as well. Please let me know within the next 10 days if you can come, as I need to book (10) ______ and plan the (11) ______ in detail. Should you need to (12) ______ me in the meantime, here's my email: everthorpe@bluecreeklabs.co.uk. Of course you can (13) ______ a call, too; should I be (14) ______ the office, one of my colleagues will take any (15) ______ calls. You can leave a message during office hours. Looking forward (16) ______ from you soon! Bye.

4 **Which is the correct word – a, b or c?**

1. She isn't here ___________ the moment.
   a) in b) on c) at
2. May I ___________ your name, please?
   a) write b) call c) take
3. How do you ___________ your name?
   a) spell b) write c) give
4. Sorry, I didn't quite ___________ that.
   a) hear b) learn c) catch
5. _______________ give you the number again just in case.
   a) I better b) I'll better c) I'd better
6. I'll ___________ he gets the message.
   a) look b) see c) watch
7. Can I make a ___________ of your number?
   a) note b) notice c) notes
8. I'll ring again ____________________.
   a) other time b) more times c) another time
9. Mr Smith will ______________ your call as soon as he gets back.
   a) return b) confirm c) repeat
10. _________________ is Fred Jones from ABC Ltd.
    a) Here b) Speaking c) This

5 **Practise using the international telephone alphabet. Write the names using Alfa, Bravo, Charlie etc.**

1. Wolfgang Whisky - Oscar - Lima - Foxtrot - Golf - Alfa - November - Golf
2. Pankratius ___________
3. Braunschweig ___________
4. Zimmermann ___________
5. Seniorenstift ___________
6. Kleinberger ___________
7. Michalsky ___________
8. Annegret ___________

Now write your name and some institutions you know using the international alphabet.

6 **Your boss is out of the office today and you're taking telephone messages from callers. Look at the example, then write down the other messages on the next page. (You can copy the Telephone Message form if you want).**

Could you tell Mr Wimmer that I enjoyed my visit to you last week and I'd like to say 'thank you' again for all his hospitality? I'm looking forward to his visit to the U.S. in May.

Telephone Message

To Mr Wimmer

Date 12 March

Time 11.45

Caller Mr Kevin Farelly

Company Bostelex Inc

Phone number 617 712-0645

Message Mr Farelly enjoyed his visit to us last week and would like to say 'thank you' again for all your hospitality. He's looking forward to your visit to the U.S. in May.

Taken by (Your name)

1. "This is Liv Ulmansson from the Swedish Medical Association. Could you please tell Mrs Jürgenbauer that I will be arriving a day late at the conference in Zurich? There are urgent matters here at our institute which I need to look after."
   "Can we possibly postpone our meeting? I hope that next Wednesday which would be the 17th is suitable for Mrs Jürgenbauer, too."
   "Just in case she needs to contact me, my phone number is 0046-77-6923-345."
2. "This is Margareta Halvorsen from Stockholm University. My telephone number is 0046-8-10 13 66."
   "Could you tell Mr Wimmer, please, that we have been given the final approval for our European nutrition research programme? That means that we can go ahead as planned and will meet here in Sweden next month."
   "Could you ask him to let me have some dates when he's free so we can arrange our meeting?"

How messages work

Remember that messages can give information or be a request:

- *Could you tell Mr Wimmer that* ... **(giving information)**
- *Could you ask Mr Wimmer to send me* ... **(request)**.

Check in your book on page 93 how you write the two sorts of telephone messages.

7 **Look at the following phone conversation, then write the complete conversation in English. Write on a separate piece of paper. Then act out the phone conversation with a partner.**

→ SB: S. 94–95

Person A	Person B
Melden Sie sich als Frau/Herr Gleiswitz, Schulleiter/in der Pankratius Grundschule in Bamberg.	Sie sind Stuart Peterson, stellvertretender Schulleiter St. Margaret's Primary School in York.
Fragen Sie, was Sie für Herrn Peterson tun können.	Sie suchen für einen Schüleraustausch eine Partnerschule in Süddeutschland. Sie haben im Internet die Homepage der Schule gesehen und würden sie gerne näher kennenlernen.
Grundsätzlich haben Sie Interesse, da Sie auch seit zwei Jahren Englisch unterrichten. Für wann ist der Austausch geplant?	Sie würden gerne im Juli des kommenden Jahres mit der ersten Gruppe kommen, im September könnte dann die deutsche Schule nach York kommen.
Die Idee hört sich gut an, Sie müssen aber erst Einzelheiten mit dem Kollegium und den Elternvertretern besprechen.	In der Zwischenzeit würden Sie gerne eine kurze englischsprachige Beschreibung der Schule erhalten, wenn das möglich ist. Selbstverständlich schicken Sie auch eine Beschreibung Ihrer Schule.
Wann sollen wir in dieser Angelegenheit wieder telefonieren? Sie bieten an in England anzurufen, wenn Ihre Vorgespräche abgeschlossen sind.	Das ist für Sie in Ordnung, wann würde das in etwa sein?
Spätestens in zwei Wochen werden Sie sich melden. Sie fragen nach der Telefonnummer.	Ländervorwahl GB 0044, dann 1904 als Vorwahl, dann die 843 283. Ihre E-Mail-Adresse ist S.peterson@margaretprimary.co.uk.
Sie bitten Herrn Peterson, das zu buchstabieren.	Sie buchstabieren die E-Mail-Adresse. Fragen Sie nach der anderen E-Mail-Adresse.
Sie geben ihre Adresse an. Gleiswitz@gs-pankratius.de.	Sie bedanken sich für das Gespräch und freuen sich, wieder aus Bamberg zu hören.
Sie verabschieden sich.	Sie verabschieden sich.

8 **Here are more role play situations. Work with a partner and make up phone calls.**

1. You work in a German retirement home. An English-speaking caller would like to make an appointment to see your retirement home because he is looking for residential care for his mother.
2. You are head nurse in a German hospital and are in charge of the intensive care unit. An English-speaking caller wants to have some information about one of your German patients. She says she is the niece living in New Zealand.
3. You call a hospital in Adelaide, Australia. You have just finished your training as a nurse in Germany and would like to spend six months working in an Australian hospital.

11 Family life and growing up

1 Complete the crossword puzzle. → SB: S. 96–97

ACROSS
3 establish, set up
6 ten years
7 termination of pregnancy
9 device intended to prevent conception
11 to become a husband or wife
12 carrying developing offspring within the body
15 take into one's family
16 having more than one wife or husband
17 husband of one's biological mother who is not one's biological father
21 knowledge acquired by learning and instruction
22 virus that causes AIDS
23 lawful
24 the period from conception to birth
26 living together as a couple without being married

DOWN
1 a legal proceeding that creates a parent-child relation between persons who are not related by blood
2 a young person between ten and 19
4 legal ending of a marriage
5 mother and father
8 relation, friendship between people
10 passed from person to person or generation to generation
13 a legally accepted relationship between a woman and a man
14 giving help and advice
18 before birth
19 a social unit living together
20 someone who cares for their children without the assistance of another parent in the home
25 people living at the same time or of approximately the same age

2 **Complete the sentences with words from the box. Then put the sentences into a logical order.**

concept • growth • delay • same-sex • values • cohabitation • traditional • patterns • generation • freedom • decades • rise • single • households • developments • divorces

1. On the one hand, this development can be seen as something positive as it reflects improvements in economic opportunities and growth in individual ________.
2. Many countries in all parts of the world have seen changes in their family ________ in the last few ________.
3. The question if marriage can mean ________ unions is being discussed in many countries.
4. Increasing numbers of women and men are choosing to remain ________.
5. People are continuing to ________ marriage.
6. For some decades, however, there have been new ________:
7. There has been a steady ________ in ________ over marriage in many industrialised countries.
8. The numbers of ________ are rising on a global scale.
9. The number of single-parent ________ has increased dramatically, too.
10. However, critics argue that we are losing traditional ________ if we give up the concept of family which has been passed on from ________ to generation.
11. For centuries the ________ family – two married parents with children – dominated our way of thinking about the ________ of family.

Order of sentences: ________

3 Have a look at the diagram below, then write a short English text explaining how the number of births and the number of women without children in Germany have changed in the last decades.

→ SB: S.102–103

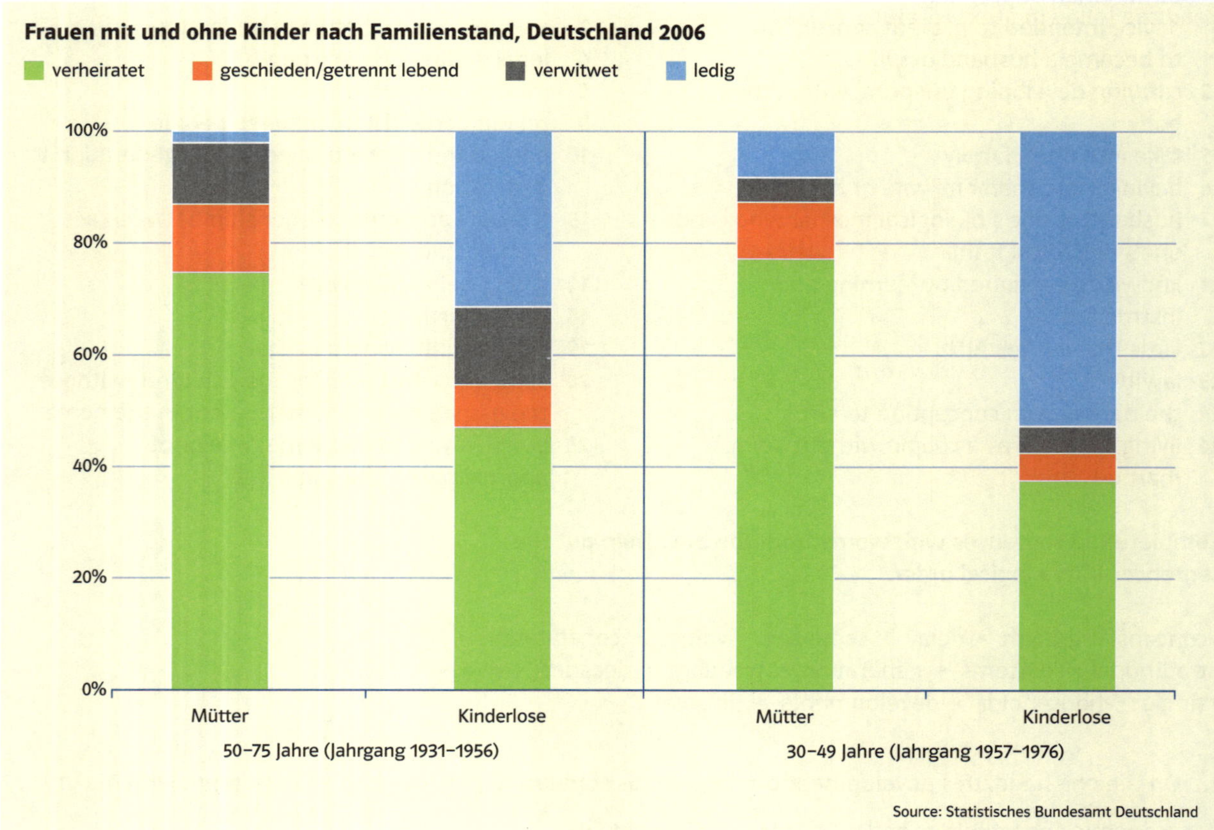

4 Write a short English text in which you summarise the following diagram.

→ SB: S.104–105

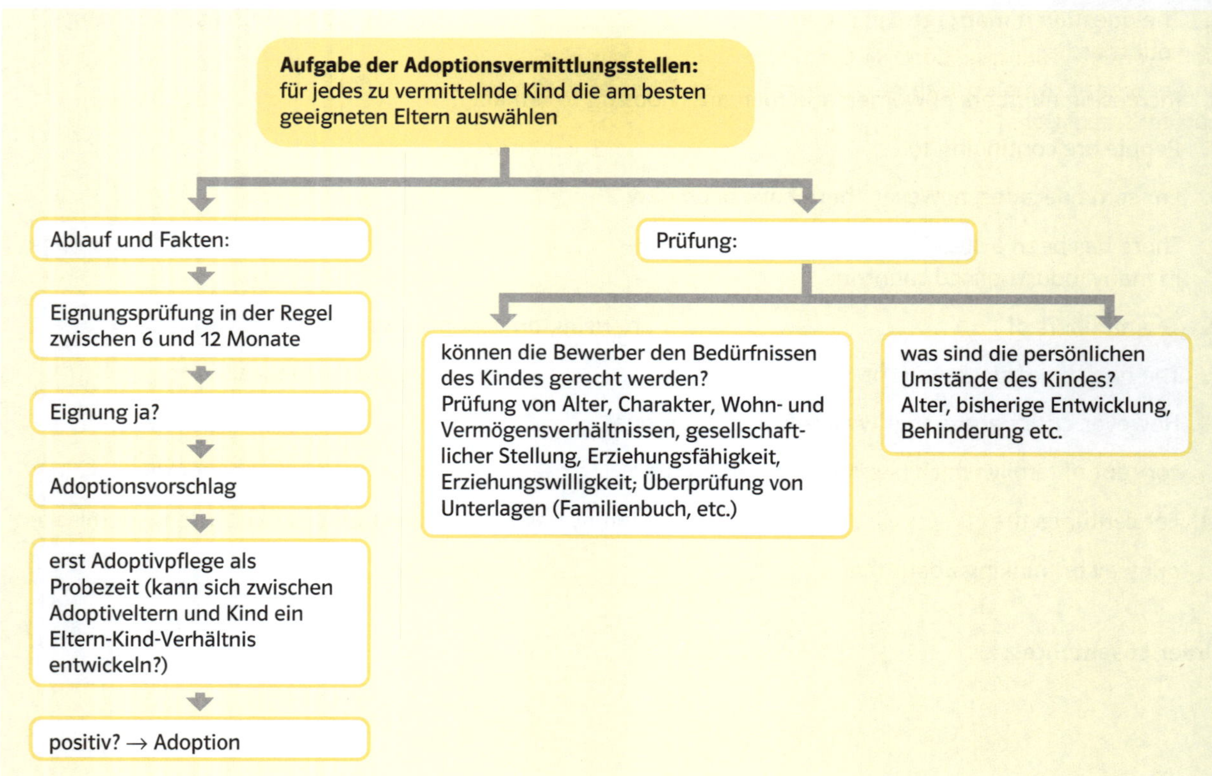

12 Dealing with other cultures

1 **Read the following text carefully, at least twice.**

→ SB: S.108–109

"Culture" is a term used every day by many people. But when asked to define what exactly they understand by the word, most of them just have vague ideas. They come up with definitions and phrases like:

- Culture describes the attitudes people share.
- Culture is something which is part of a nation but yet is different from nationality.
- Culture represents whatever is characteristic of a society at a given time and place.
- Culture is the knowledge and values shared by a society.

These ideas seem to suggest that culture is a concept uniting people. However, many countries agree that they consist of many cultures, that they are multicultural. This, on the other hand, means that these different cultures face the challenge of coexisting in a peaceful and respectful way, with none of the cultures claiming to be superior.

This demand, however, is rejected by traditionalists and conservative political leaders, who claim that over centuries countries have developed their own culture. This culture is reflected in an established set of values, beliefs and attitudes. Therefore, they say, there is a historical justification for the concept of a leading culture. Opponents to this idea argue that culture refers to something in a society that is constantly changing and adapting to new circumstances. Therefore, in their opinion, there is no such thing as a German, a British or an American culture which can be characterised over centuries by the same ideas and values.

2 **Now work out four questions on the text to ask your partner. Remember to come up with model answers, too. Then answer your partner's questions.**

Question 1: ______________________________

Model answer: ______________________________

____

Question 2: ______________________________

Model answer: ______________________________

____

Question 3: ______________________________

Model answer: ______________________________

____

Question 4: ______________________________

Model answer: ______________________________

____

____

3 Collect arguments for and against the following statements on school culture and write them down below.

→ SB: S. 110–111

	For	Against
1 Schools should be open from 7 am to 9 pm; every teacher should be present and available at least 9 hours every day.		

	For	Against
2 Students who clearly say that they do not want to learn and get a degree should be expelled immediately.		

	For	Against
3 Every school in Germany should provide school lunch.		

	For	Against
4 Teachers should get school certificates from their students.		

5 There should be school uniforms at German schools.	For	Against

4 **Summarise the following diagram about the NHS (National Health Service) in German.**

→ SB: S. 112–113

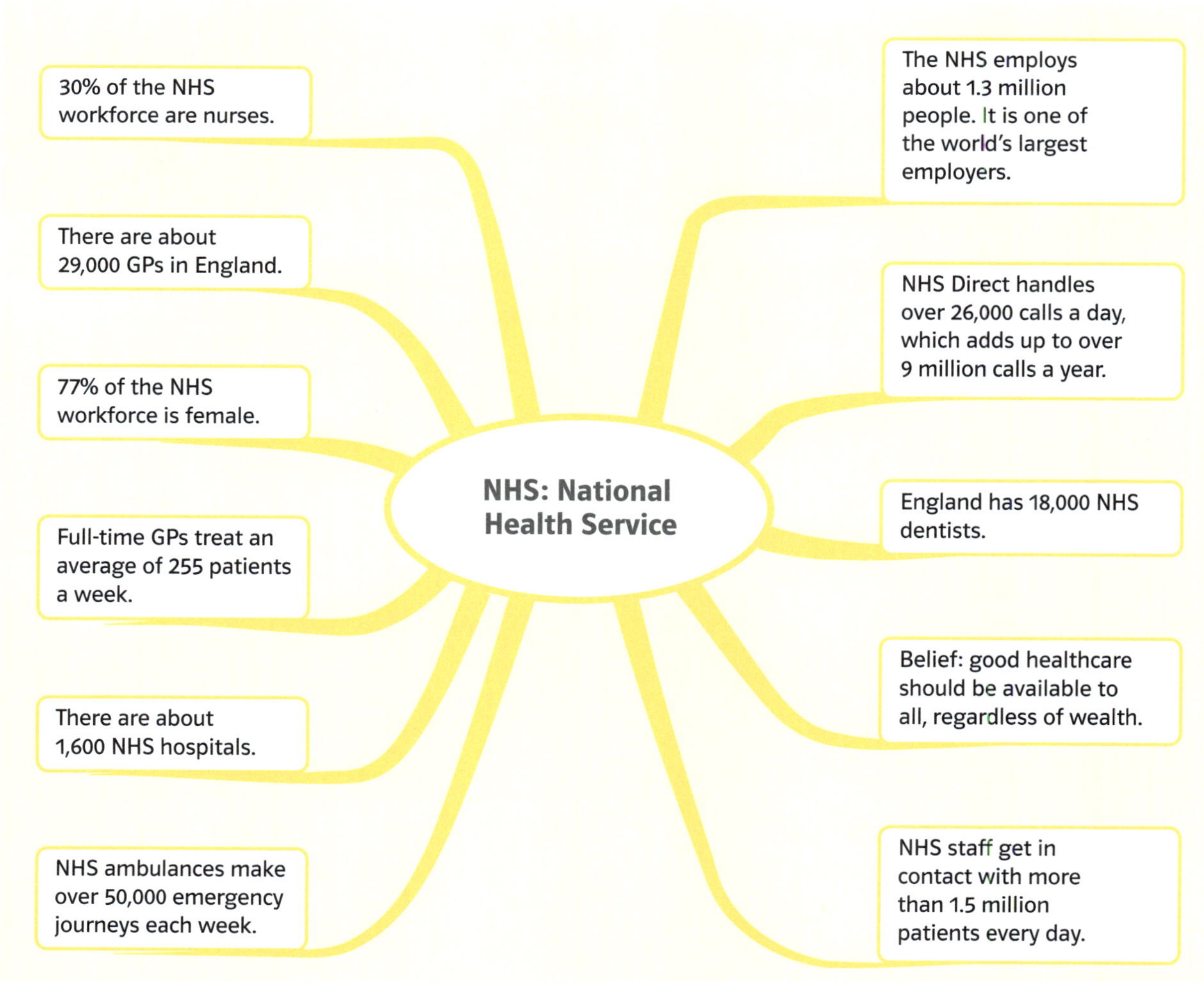

13 Dealing with the media

1 **Arrange the words in categories. Use the three categories given below and add further categories. Find more words to complete the categories. Talk with a partner about your categories and your vocabulary.**

→ SB: S.114–115

print media • advertising • mass media

internet | witness | target | electronic

website | report | publicity | famous

advertisement | interest | online | the public

journalist | curiosity | budget | sensational

censor | blog | podcast | protection | privacy

paparazzi | freelancer | celebrities | newspaper

brochure | leaflet | communication | control

influence | magazine | inform | entertain

content | viewpoint

Category:	**Category:**

Category:	Category:

Category:	Category:

2 Find the odd one out. Prepare to give reasons for your decisions.

1. journalist – reporter – writer – paparazzo ____________________
2. text – story – report – brochure ____________________
3. entertain – inform – influence – advertise ____________________
4. website – leaflet – brochure – newspaper ____________________
5. blog – podcast – website – magazine ____________________
6. freelancer – reporter – celebrity – paparazzi ____________________
7. interesting – sensational – new – entertaining ____________________
8. control – restrict – limit – censor ____________________

3 Work with a partner. Use the vocabulary of unit 13 and make your own list of words including one odd one out. Now show your list to your partner and ask him/her to find the odd one out.

4 **Reporting what people have said. Muriel Kammeier works for MediPool GmbH, an advertising agency for private clinics and health service providers. Yesterday, at a conference in Copenhagen, she gave a presentation about the rise in cosmetic surgery in various European countries. What did she say? Finish the sentences below.**

→ SB: S.116–117, GS: E

1. Cosmetic surgery is no longer reserved for celebrities. The procedures are now much more affordable and available than in the past.

Muriel said that cosmetic surgery was no longer reserved for celebrities.

2. Over the last decade, prices for even the most complicated surgery have dropped.

She said ______

3. Another factor adding to the popularity of cosmetic surgery is that most procedures are now much safer and quicker.

Muriel told the listeners that ______

4. People aged 35–50 have the most procedures. This target group normally has the financial means to pay for the surgery.

Moreover she mentioned that ______

5. References from former patients and open-house events are the best way to find customers. These advertising campaigns are also much less costly.

She mentioned that ______

6. Experts agree that it is very important to inform the patients about possible side effects of plastic surgery. A website with links to all kinds of documentation is an inexpensive way to reach your target group.

______

7. Critics argue that people need to accept the way they look. They say that buying plastic surgery like buying household appliances is a dangerous trend.

9. This trend will in the long run ruin the good image plastic surgery has been able to create in recent years.

8. Reports say that especially teenagers are very much in danger of regarding their bodies as a collection of spare parts *(Ersatzteile)*.

10. Advertising and marketing campaigns should therefore focus on health aspects and factual information.

Analysing advertisements

When you want to analyse an advertisement, you need to think of the following things.

- What is the product or service that is being advertised?
- What is the advertising medium (e.g. a poster, an internet pop-up)?
- Who is the ad targeting – what is the product's target group – men, women, older people, … ?
- What image of the product does the ad try to give – healthy, hi-tech, 'exclusive', not expensive, …
- How does it try to do this – what 'devices' *(Instrumente)* does it use? Think of pictures, text and layout. An ad can be very complicated (with lots of text) or very simple. It can use humour. It can have lots of 'white space' …
- What do you think of the ad yourself – what reaction(s) do you have to it? Do you find it successful? Awful (for example, you may find it sexist or silly). Is it clever? Remember – it targets a specific group, and you may not be in that group!

5 **One of the most important parts of an advertisement will be the brand image of the product. List as many words and phrases as you can that describe products or services. Use your dictionary if necessary.** → SB: S. 118–119

healthy, hi-tech, exclusive, not expensive (cheap)

Video lounge

→ SB: S.123, Schüler DVD V5, Schüler DVD Videotext

1 **Before you watch the video, look through the background information and the useful expressions below.**

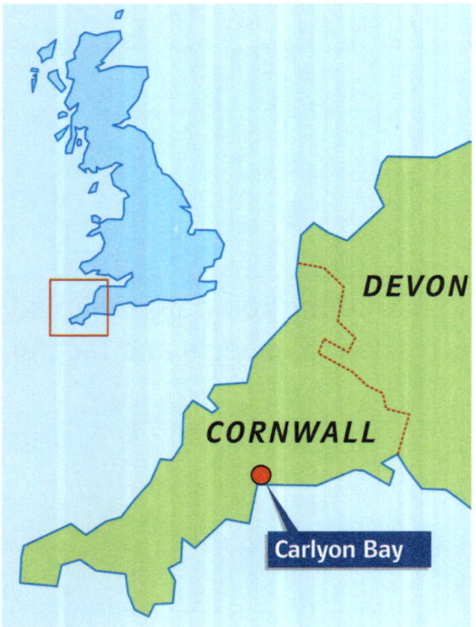

Hadley Centre for Climate Prediction
A UK government organisation that studies how global warming is affecting the UK.

'Planning struggles'
A company that wants to build for example a new hotel must first get planning permission *(Baugenehmigung)*. Sometimes there are vigorous objections *(gravierende Einsprüche)* and that can lead to a struggle *(Kampf)*. If the problem is really bad, there can be a public enquiry *(öffentliche Untersuchung)*. It will look at both sides and pass judgement *(ein Urteil sprechen)*.

Useful expressions

scorcher *sehr heißer Tag*
lure *Verlockung*
to devise *ausarbeiten, formulieren*
to set (to change) *(hier) wird sich bald ändern*
influx *Einströmen*
prediction *Voraussage*
picture (v.) *(hier) Stellen Sie sich … vor*
to spring up *(plötzlich) erscheinen*
prospect *Aussicht*
to cope (with sth.) *(etw.) bewältigen*
clogged *verkehrsreich, verstopft*
to put strain on sth. *etw. belasten*
waste *(hier) Abfallentsorgung*
relentless *unablässig*

2 **Before you watch the video, have a close look at the following statements.**

a ☐ Millions travel for a guarantee of warm weather.
b ☐ By 2050, the Mediterranean will have become too hot for tourism.
c ☐ In 2050 the British coastline will come under relentless pressure.
d ☐ Local people in places like Cornwall welcome this development, however they do have worries.
e ☐ The mass influx of tourism means a lot of opportunities but also a strain of the health service, the water supply and the transport system.
f ☐ Cornwall would be dead without the people bringing the money in.
g ☐ The traditional image of the British seafront faces transformation.
h ☐ Millions of people will head to the UK for their holidays.

Now watch the video and number the statements in the order in which they appear.

3 **Watch the video again and add further aspects which are important.**

____
____
____
____
____
____

4 **Now write a short German summary of the video using your notes.**

14 Working as a volunteer abroad

1 Complete the crossword puzzle based on vocabulary from unit 14. Expressions consisting of two words (i.e. partner agency) take a blank between the two words.

→ SB: S.126–128

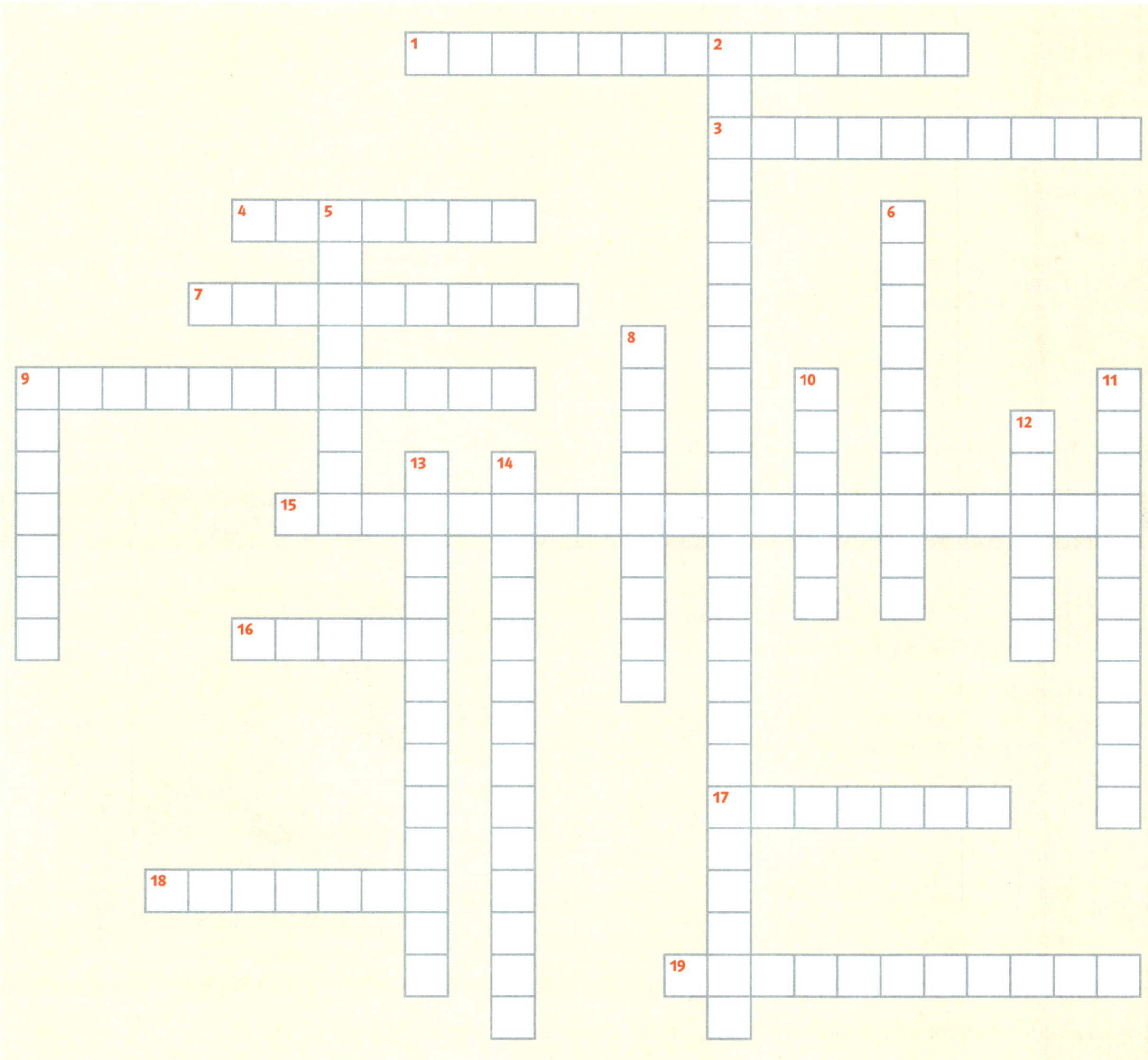

ACROSS
- **1** Unterkunft
- **3** Freiwillige
- **4** Armut
- **7** Herausforderung
- **9** Umweltschutz
- **15** Entwicklungsländer
- **16** Thema
- **17** Unterstützung
- **18** zur Verfügung stellen
- **19** Arbeitserlaubnis

DOWN
- **2** Entwicklungsorganisation
- **5** wertvoll
- **6** Erfahrung
- **8** Stärken
- **9** Wohlfahrt
- **10** im Ausland
- **11** Spenden beschaffen
- **12** Fähigkeiten
- **13** Gesundheitsuntersuchung
- **14** Freiwilligenarbeit

2 **Fill in the table with words from the same word family and say what word class you have chosen.**

	Word from same word family	Word class
permit	to permit	verb
guidance	to guide	verb
to contribute		
to apply		
valuable		
experience		
to check		
to volunteer		
poverty		
to fight		

	Word from same word family	Word class
developing		
capability		
awareness		
restoration		
organisation		
education		
applicant		
to decide		
to renovate		
repair		

3 **Going abroad. You have been offered the following placement.**

DO YOU LIKE TO WORK IN A NURSERY SCHOOL IN UGANDA?

We take care of children whose parents have died from AIDS. The placement is under inspection of the WHO.

More details:
- stay for six months, stay longer if you wish
- free basic accommodation
- visas and flights will be paid
- you will just need $150 a month for food

You will form a team with an African student. And you could begin directly after you have finished school.

Collect arguments for and against this placement and arrange them from strongest to weaker.

Volunteering to work in Uganda

For	**Against**

15 Food and health

1 **Work through the text and summarise the most important ideas in German.**

→ SB: S. 132–133

EVERY year millions of people try new and revolutionary diets and methods for losing weight. They spend billions on new promises made by the advertising industry to get closer to the ideal figure in a matter of weeks. But all too often they are disappointed when the new diet does not work miracles.

The secret to weight loss is as simple as it is logical: you just need to eat healthily and get some exercise, thus burning more calories than you take in!

Here are some more detailed tips for losing weight which are realistic and easy to follow:

- Set realistic goals for your weight loss. Small steps lead to success as well.
- Have breakfast every morning. Breakfast is the most important meal of the day so allow at least 20 minutes for a good healthy breakfast.
- Run or walk every day. Running is a great way to get in shape. You will both drop extra pounds and your body will gain extra muscle. Don't get frustrated if you can't run five miles without stopping to begin with; take a break as often as you need to.

- Find someone to join you in your daily exercise. It is more fun with a partner. If you cannot convince a family member or friend, ask your dog.
- Drink lots of water. Health experts recommend at least 2 litres a day. Do not replace water by coke, coffee or juices. They either dehydrate your body or they are rich in sugar and calories.
- Eat slowly so that you will not overeat. Allow your stomach to give a signal to the brain that you have eaten enough.
- Have a proper meal every day so that you do not go to bed hungry.
- Don't eat just because you are bored. If you don't know what to do, get some exercise.

2 **Talk about the tips in the text with a partner and agree on your top ten ideas on how to lose weight.**

1. ______________________________
2. ______________________________
3. ______________________________
4. ______________________________
5. ______________________________
6. ______________________________
7. ______________________________
8. ______________________________
9. ______________________________
10. ______________________________

3 Collect arguments for and against the following statements.

1 There should be more dieticians so that all of us can get dietary advice.	Yes, I absolutely agree because ...	No, I'm afraid I do not agree because ...

2 People who do not live in a healthy way should have to pay more for their health insurance.	Yes, I absolutely agree because ...	No, I'm afraid I do not agree because ...

3 Everybody should accept themselves the way they are.	Yes, I absolutely agree because ...	No, I'm afraid I do not agree because ...

4 Fitness and healthy living are extremely important for those under 30.	Yes, I absolutely agree because ...	No, I'm afraid I do not agree because ...

5 It is a good idea to have role models who look fit and slim.	Yes, I absolutely agree because ...	No, I'm afraid I do not agree because ...

Video lounge

→ SB: S.141, Schüler DVD V6, Schüler DVD Videotext

1 **Before you watch the video about sexually transmitted infections (STI), discuss the following statements with a partner.**

Condoms should be handed out for free.

It is better not to have sex until you get married.

Sexually transmitted infections are not a big issue among today's teenagers.

2 **Now watch the video and complete the table with information from the film.**

Young people and STIs	
STIs: facts and consequences	
Going abroad: travel and STIs	
Medical services in the UK	
Government action	

3 **In the video Jessica says that she does not really know a lot about sexually transmitted infections. Write an email to her in which you give her some advice on how to behave.**

16 Applying for a job

1 **Read about this German student called Natascha Zellweg. Then look at the advertisement and complete the grid below in German.**

→ SB: S.144–145

Natascha Zellweg is a student at a vocational college in Bielefeld. She is in the second year of a two-year full-time Health and Social Science course. She hopes to become a *Erzieherin* – a nursery nurse.

Before beginning work, Natascha would like to do a 6-month work placement in an English-speaking country and right now she's looking at an advertisement in a student magazine called Life Abroad. Natascha thinks that she'd like to apply for the placement.

GES Kindergarten London Ltd

GES

We at GES (German English speaking) Kindergarten in London are looking for an intern to assist us in our daily work here at our nursery school. Founded in 2002, we are a rapidly growing institution for currently 27 children.

Four qualified nursery teachers look after the children, aged three to five. The official language at our kindergarten is German. However, all our staff are fluent in both languages and encourage the children to use both languages.

We are looking for an intern who has both qualifications and experience in working with children. We expect a good command of German and English. The successful applicant will be at least 18 years old and a good team player.

We will assist you in finding affordable accommodation in London. Breakfast and lunch will be provided at work. We pay £240 a month. The minimum stay is 6 months.
If you are interested, please apply in writing to Ms Moira Sutcliffe (manager), Old Street 22, EC1 9JH London, UK.

Land/Stadt	Großbritannien / London
Art des Unternehmens	
Art der Tätigkeit(en)	
Voraussetzungen	
Bezahlung	
Unterkunft	
Name der Kontaktperson	

2 Natascha wrote the letter of application below. In the box, there is some extra information about Natascha. Use all the information you have about Natascha and the advertisement to complete the letter. Remember to use the correct layout for a formal personal letter.

→ SB: S. 146–147

Address: Walkenweg 17, 33605 Bielefeld, Germany
Work experience: completed a 4-week work placement last year
Hobbies: ice skating

(1) ______________________
____
____

(2) ______________________
____
____
____

4 February 20 __

(3) ______________________

(4) ______________________

I would like to apply for the internship which you advertised in the magazine

(5) ______________ of 3 February.

I am currently in the second year of (6) ______________________
______________________ at a vocational college in (7) ______________,
Germany. At the end of the course I will obtain my 'Fachhochschulreife' qualification.

I hope to become (8) ______________________
______________________.

As you will see from my enclosed CV, I have excellent computer skills and a good knowledge of English (B2 Level in the Common European Framework). As part of my college course last year, I successfully completed (9) ______________________.

I have a wide range of interests including (10) ______________________.

I would very much welcome the opportunity to work at GES kindergarten in London and believe that I would be a valuable and enthusiastic employee. I hope that you will consider my application and look forward to hearing from you.

(11) ______________________

Natascha Zellweg

Natascha Zellweg

(12) ______________________

3 **Use the suitable English phrases.**

Nesrin Yüksel, a student in Cologne, is also applying for a work placement at the moment. The placement is for six months in a hotel in Canada and she saw the advertisement for it online.

Nesrin has made some notes in German about what she would like to say in her letter of application. Write in the English phrases that she can use.

1. Sehr geehrter Herr MacKenzie,
   Dear Mr MacKenzie
2. ich möchte mich auf die auf der Canada Tourism Website ausgeschriebene Praktikumsstelle bewerben.
3. Zurzeit bin ich im zweiten Jahr eines zweijährigen Kurses an einer berufsbildenden Schule in Köln, Deutschland.
4. Wie aus meinem Lebenslauf zu ersehen ist, verfüge ich über gute Englisch- und Computerkenntnisse.
5. Ich bin fleißig, lernwillig und ein kommunikativer Mensch.
6. Ich verfüge bereits über Berufserfahrung im Hotelwesen *(in the hotel industry)*. Letztes Jahr habe ich in meinen Sommerferien in einem internationalen Hotel in der Türkei gearbeitet.
7. In meiner Freizeit interessiere ich mich u. a. für Sport, Musik und Tanzen.
8. Über die Möglichkeit, in einem kanadischen Hotel zu arbeiten, würde ich mich sehr freuen.
9. Ich hoffe, dass Sie meine Bewerbung in Betracht ziehen, und freue mich auf Ihre Antwort.
10. Mit freundlichen Grüßen,

4 Now YOU.

→ SB: S.148–149

- **Read the advertisement below. Copy the grid on page 54 and complete it in German with information about the placements.**
- **Write an email to apply for a placement. Give your own details and use today's date.**
- **Attach your current CV.**

praktikumsbörse.de → Praktika im Ausland

Work placement in children's home in Sri Lanka

Give Hope Ltd. is an international organisation running children's homes in Sri Lanka. For one of our children's homes in Marawila on the west coast we are looking for friendly and enthusiastic students who would like to spend some time in a home for girls aged 4 to 16.

What we offer:
- a monthly salary of €320
- flight to Sri Lanka
- transfer to Marawila
- accommodation in double room (to be shared with another student)
- free meals in children's home

These would be your main duties:
- two English lessons a day in which you teach the girls the alphabet, vocabulary, and simple sentences
- games and creative activities for and with the girls
- maintaining a blog on the internet in which you report about your placement

What we expect:
- a good knowledge of English
- computer skills
- experience in working with children of that age group
- affection and empathy for children
- patience and understanding
- minimum age 18

The placement should be for between 4 and 12 months. You can start at anytime. There are three positions for students available. To apply, please send an email including CV and letter of application to info@givehope.org. We will contact you with further details of the placements.

5 **Here are some of the keywords from Unit 16. Use them to complete the sentences.**

a good communicator • a good knowledge of English • advertised • advertisement • applicant • wage • application • currently • hard working • internship • keen to learn • reliable • ~~to apply~~ • unpaid

1. When you want to apply for a job or a work placement, you write a letter of ________.
2. A person who applies for a job is an ________.
3. Another word for a work placement is an ________.
4. People often find out about jobs or work placements when they see an ________ online or in a newspaper.
5. Letters often begin with the words: 'I would like to apply for the work placement which you ________ on the Praktikumsbörse website'.
6. Another word for 'at the moment' is ________.
7. Employers often say that they are looking for people who are ________, ________, ________ and ________.
8. ________ is also often essential.
9. Some work placements are ________ *(unbezahlt)*, but sometimes people also receive a ________.

Practice exam 1

★ Esther Wilms, 20, lives in Bonn. She has just finished a two-year course in health and social care at the local vocational college. Since her uncle works as a doctor at a hospital in Grand Rapids, USA, Esther has decided that she would like to spend some time abroad before beginning a traineeship in Germany.
Her parents have agreed to pay for her flight; her uncle has invited Esther to stay with him and his family.

A1.27 Teil 1 REZEPTION mündlich (Hörverstehen)

★ In the meantime, Esther has contacted her uncle and asked him for help in finding a place to work. She has told him about her two-year course at the vocational college and that she would most like to do some work which involves dealing with children and/or teenagers. When she comes home, she finds the following message on her answerphone.

YOUR TASK Listen to the message and fill in the information on the message pad.

Caller's name ____________________

Institution ____________________

Reason for calling ____________________

____

____

____

____

____

Information about internship / institution ____________________

____

____

____

____

____

Further information ____________________

____

____

____

____

Teil 2 MEDIATION

★ Esther has written back to Nancy confirming her stay at CCC in Grand Rapids. Now she decides to prepare for her time in the USA and has another look at some of the papers from her course at the vocational college. In her final year, her class carried out a survey on eating habits among children and teenagers in Bonn. As the local newspaper published an article about their project, Esther decides that she would like to be able to tell the staff at CCC about this survey.

YOUR TASK Work through the following German newspaper article and summarise its main parts in English.

Umfrage der 12BFS3 am Konrad-Adenauer-Berufskolleg zu Ess- und Trinkgewohnheiten bei Kindern und Jugendlichen

Die Klasse 12BFS3 des Konrad-Adenauer-Berufskollegs Bonn führte vor den Sommerferien ein einwöchiges Projekt zu Ess- und Trinkgewohnheiten von Kindern und Jugendlichen durch. Im Rahmen des Projekts nahmen die Berufskollegschüler Kontakt zu insgesamt sechs Grundschulklassen, sechs Haupt- und vier Realschulklassen, sowie fünf Gymnasial- und acht Berufskollegklassen auf. Das Alter der Befragten war zwischen sieben und 25 Jahre, insgesamt konnten die Schüler und die begleitenden Lehrer ca. 450 Fragebögen auswerten. Dies sind die wichtigsten Ergebnisse:

Die befragten Kinder und Jugendlichen gaben in der Befragung an, dass sie relativ selten Fast Food und Fleisch essen und regelmäßig Milch trinken. Dies war für die Klasse eine sehr positive Überraschung, da sie ihre Erwartungen anderes formuliert hatten.

Dass die Schülerinnen und Schüler mit ihren eher pessimistischen Annahmen über das Ess- und Trinkverhalten zum Teil doch Recht hatten, zeigt sich darin, dass der Anteil von Jugendlichen, der ein- bis zweimal pro Woche oder häufiger Fast Food konsumiert, mit zunehmendem Alter stark zunimmt. Etwa ein Drittel der 14- bis 17-Jährigen isst mindestens einmal pro Woche Fast Food. In dieser Altersgruppe isst auch jeder Dritte mehrmals in der Woche Fertiggerichte.

Eine große Mehrheit der Befragten isst im Vergleich zu den Empfehlungen der DGE zu häufig Wurst und Süßigkeiten. Fisch, Gemüse und frisches Obst sind nicht so beliebt, wie sie sein sollten. Beliebt sind dagegen leider süße Nahrungsmittel: jeder fünfte Befragte isst täglich Schokolade oder andere Süßigkeiten. Bei den Jungen sind zusätzlich Softdrinks und Energydrinks beliebt; der Anteil der Personen, die täglich bzw. mehrmals täglich Softdrinks zu sich nimmt, steigt mit zunehmendem Alter.

Etwa die Hälfte der Jungen und Mädchen in der Umfrage verzehrt zwar mindestens einmal täglich Obst, jedoch weniger als empfohlen (man sollte das mehrmals tun!). Wie schon beim Fast Food gilt auch hier: Je älter die Jugendlichen werden, umso weniger gesund ernähren sie sich. Brot wird insgesamt relativ häufig gegessen, Weißbrot und Brötchen sind aber beliebter als Vollkornbrot.

Insgesamt stellten die Schülerinnen und Schüler bei ihren Auswertungen fest, dass sich bei den Jugendlichen mit zunehmendem Alter das Ernährungsverhalten verschlechtert, sich aber auch dann noch die Mädchen insgesamt etwas ausgewogener ernähren als die Jungen. Zum Abschluss des Projekts wurden die Ergebnisse mit wissenschaftlichen Texten und Studien abgeglichen. Zwar sind die Bonner Ergebnisse nicht in allen Einzelheiten identisch mit den Ergebnissen für deutsche Kinder und Jugendliche im Durchschnitt, es gibt aber sehr viele Gemeinsamkeiten.

Auch wenn nicht alle Ergebnisse froh stimmen: ein großes Kompliment für die Arbeit dieser Schulklasse!

Teil 3 REZEPTION Leseverstehen

★ Esther has sent Nancy Erlbaum yet another email giving her an outline of the project they did at school. Nancy in return sends the following information.

YOUR TASK Read Nancy's mail and complete the table on the next page in English.

Dear Esther

As promised, I am sending you some information about CCC and our neighborhood in general.
CCC is a government-based neighborhood center. Our task is to provide assistance and special advice for the people living in the area.

As I said already, at present the focus clearly lies on childcare, educational classes and health-related issues. Even though Ciderwood cannot be called a deprived neighborhood, we clearly see an increased demand for classes like this. Like many other US neighborhoods, Ciderwood has experienced some economic problems due to the closing of some car factories two years ago. Currently, the unemployment rate is 2% above the national average.

As you have shown quite an interest in nutrition and eating habits, let me give you a brief outline of the situation here in our area.
In terms of nutrition, Ciderwood is witnessing the same developments that are visible in most of the USA. Even though there is enough evidence that teenagers from deprived neighborhoods are more prone to obesity, some behavioural patterns occur all over the USA and of course all over Grand Rapids:

- About 10 in 100 young American women suffer from eating disorders. Since 1980, the number of overweight children in the USA has doubled.
- The eating habits of teenagers are characterized by skipping meals, routine fast food consumption, frequent snacking and dieting.
- More than half of male teens and more than two-thirds of female teens do not eat breakfast on a regular basis. Irregular schedules, convenience, work and social activities are the main reasons teenagers give for skipping meals.
- Fast food has increasingly replaced regular eating patterns. It is convenient and typically a social affair. Mostly teenagers are unaware of the fact that by consuming too much fast food they receive the majority of their calories as empty calories from processed and high-fat foods.

On the other hand teens often diet because "Thin is in". Due to the fact that more and more teenagers do not know how to keep a healthy diet, this is where the vicious circle of fast food and dieting starts.

We try to help them by giving them the following advice:

- Be active!
- Adults should be physically active for at least 30 minutes a day, children for at least 60 minutes.

- Regular family meals result in better eating habits.
- Know what you eat!
- Eat lean cuts, seafood and beans. Avoid frying. Eat low-fat or fat-free dairy products. Consume a variety of fruits but do not drink too much juice. Vary the types of vegetables you eat. Half of all the grains consumed should be whole grains.
- Make fast food an exception!
- Fast food may well be sociable and convenient, but it does not give the body what it needs when you consume too much of it.

That is my brief outline of our situation here at CCC.

I hope that we will be in touch again soon.

Best regards,
Nancy

Aspect	Information from the text
CCC	
Ciderwood area	
Eating behaviour US teens	
Advice given by CCC	

Teil 4 PRODUKTION schriftlich

(Verfassen eines englischsprachigen Berichts nach Stichworten)

★ Shortly before Esther prepares to leave for the US, Nancy contacts her again. As she is now planning a detailed schedule for Esther's first weeks, she asks her to write a short report about her job-related work experience and activities in health and social care.

YOUR TASK Write Esther's report about her job-related activities based on her notes.

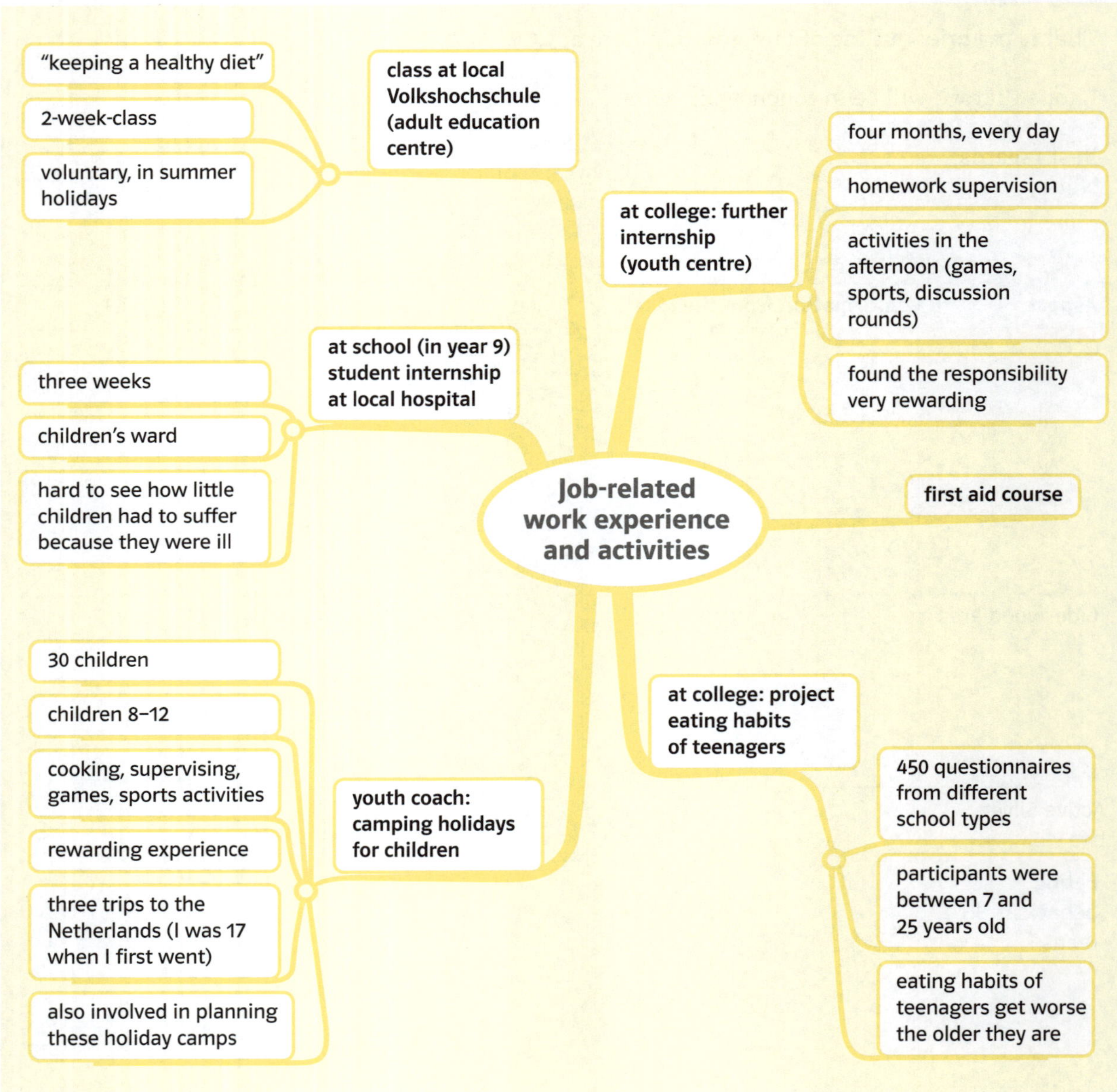

Teil 5 PRODUKTION eigene Stellungnahme

★ In one of Nancy Erlbaum's emails to Esther, she says: "Sometimes I wish they would treat fast food like they treat alcohol and tobacco. There should be a law making it illegal for teenagers under 14 to buy fast food if they are not accompanied by their parents or other adults."

YOUR TASK Comment on Nancy's statement. Give reasons for your opinion.

Practice exam 2

★ Fiona Katzenberg is a registered nurse for the elderly. Born in Bremen 24 years ago, Fiona now lives and works in New Plymouth, New Zealand. In this little town on the west coast of New Zealand's northern island, Fiona has a job in New Plymouth Meadows Park, a retirement community for about 250 residents. New Plymouth Meadows Park is one of eleven retirement villages run by Active Silver Life, New Zealand's leading operator of retirement villages.

A1.28

Teil 1 REZEPTION mündlich (Hörverstehen)

★ Before Fiona chose New Plymouth as her new home, all she knew was that she wanted to go to New Zealand and work there for a couple of years. A friend of hers who knew about Fiona's professional background and already lived in that part of the world sent her the following radio programme about Active Silver Life, which set the ball rolling.

YOUR TASK Listen to the radio programme and fill in the relevant information.

Aspect	Information from the radio programme
general information about Active Silver Life	
Active Silver Life villages	
Assisted living means …	

★ As Fiona found the information about Active Silver Life very interesting, she had a look at the job vacancies the company was trying to fill. In the following job advertisement, Active Silver Life was looking for registered nurses, a position Fiona had already worked in back in Bremen.

YOUR TASK Work through the job advertisement below and answer the following questions in German.

1. Welche fachlichen und personalen Anforderungen stellt Active Silver Life an die Bewerber?
2. Geben Sie kurz in eigenen Worten die Stellenbeschreibung wieder.
3. Was bietet Active Silver Life?

Registered Nurse

As an experienced registered nurse, you know how to care for other people – now here's an opportunity to care for yourself and your career as well.

Our team at Active Silver Life has two vacancies for a full-time Registered Nurse. We need two skilled geriatric care experts to complete our motivated teams in our retirement villages in New Plymouth and Christchurch.

If you are a committed Registered Nurse with at least 5 years experience in eldercare and are looking for a great team to work with and a great company to provide you with job satisfaction, please read on!

Active Silver Life is New Zealand's leading operator of retirement villages. As one of the key players in eldercare in this country we are proud to be able to provide the supportive working environment you have always dreamed of. This is what we offer:

- a wide range of modern, state-of-the-art facilities
- competitive pay
- a personal and lasting relationship with the people you care for
- ample opportunities for professional development
- a free, comfortable 2-bedroom on-site apartment
- the opportunity to join the market leader in retirement care

Active Silver Life in New Plymouth and Christchurch is looking for two full-time Registered Nurses to work 38 hours per week including two Saturdays and Sundays a month. We offer the highest standards of eldercare in a supportive team environment. Active Silver Life offers professional development opportunities and a competitive pay which reflect your skills and experience.
Currently our team is looking for two nurses to work flexible shifts including weekends. Your ability to communicate and your experienced capacity to care will make your work at Active Silver Life rewarding for both you and our residents. You will be part of a friendly team and will have the opportunity for further training, giving you the chance to grow, learn and develop.

Are you ready to make the move to a place where professional challenge and job satisfaction go hand in hand?
Are you willing and prepared to accept responsibility?
Are you familiar with the latest developments in geriatric care?
Are you patient and calm, yet committed to caring for older people?
Are you an outstanding team player?
Are you the one we are looking for?

For further details about Active Silver Life or questions regarding your application, please turn to:

Margaret Scarborough,
Personnel Manager Active Silver Life
m.scarborough@activesilverlife.co.nz

Teil 3 MEDIATION

★ When Fiona started her job at New Plymouth Meadows Park, her employer Active Silver Life promised her training on the job. In one of the seminars on recent developments in geriatric care that Fiona has attended so far, the other participants asked her to give a short outline of the situation of the elderly in Germany. On the internet she finds the following article on an aging German society and possible consequences for eldercare systems.

YOUR TASK **Work through the following German article and summarise its main parts in English.**

Die Deutschen leben in einer schrumpfenden und vergreisenden Gesellschaft. Nach aktuellen Berechnungen wird die Bevölkerungszahl bis zum Jahr 2030 um ca. 1,2 Mio. abnehmen, bis zum Jahr 2050 verringert sie sich auf knapp 74 Mio. Gleichzeitig wird die Bevölkerung immer älter. Im Jahr 2000 war das Durchschnittsalter der Deutschen 38 Jahre, im Jahr 2050 wird jeder zweite Mann älter als 51 und jede zweite Frau älter als 53 Jahre sein. Der Anteil der Rentner wird kontinuierlich ansteigen; die über 65-Jährigen werden sich bis 2050 prozentual mehr als verdoppeln. Der Anteil der über 80-Jährigen wird sich von heute bis zum Jahr 2050 verdreifachen, im Jahr 2065 werden 115 000 Menschen über 100 Jahre alt sein.

Der größere Teil alter Menschen sieht das Alter als einen Gewinn an Lebensqualität; sowohl soziale Beziehungen, finanzielle Situation sowie das Leben insgesamt werden weitgehend positiv bewertet. Aktiv sein charakterisiert nach eigenen Worten das Leben der Rentner mehr als Nichtstun.

Dennoch erhöht die allgemeine Lebenszeitverlängerung unweigerlich die Zunahme von chronischen Krankheiten. Jeder fünfte über 65-Jährige leidet an einer dauerhaften Erkrankung oder Behinderung, jeder dritte über 70-Jährige hat fünf verschiedene Krankheiten. Insgesamt nutzen alte Frauen und Männer zunehmend Gesundheits- und Pflegeleistungen.

Daraus ergibt sich, dass die Pflegebranche ein Wirtschaftszweig mit steigenden Beschäftigungszahlen ist. Ende 2007 waren etwa 4,4 Millionen Menschen im Gesundheitswesen tätig, besonders im Bereich der ambulanten Pflege gab es einen deutlich erhöhten Stellenzuwachs. Dieser Trend wird auch in den nächsten Jahren und Jahrzehnten anhalten, da auf Grund der steigenden Lebenserwartung auch die Anzahl kranker und pflegebedürftiger Menschen deutlich zunehmen wird. Vom Gesundheits- und Pflegesystem wird mehr Leistung gefordert werden, jedoch wird der sich für die Zukunft abzeichnende Fachkräftemangel in einigen Bereichen und Regionen schon jetzt spürbar.

Hinsichtlich der Arbeitsbedingungen gilt die Pflegebranche bereits heute als hoch belastet. Wenig attraktive Arbeitsbedingungen und oft zu geringe Bezahlung verstärken jedoch den Mangel an qualifizierten Nachwuchskräften. Viele Experten sind sich aber einig in der Einschätzung, dass eine der wesentlichen Aufgaben einer alternden Gesellschaft darin besteht, die personellen Ressourcen für die Pflege für die nächsten Jahre und Jahrzehnte bereitzustellen. Noch nie war es so wichtig, eine ausreichende Anzahl junger Menschen für die medizinischen, pflegerischen und therapeutischen Berufe zu gewinnen.

Teil 4 PRODUKTION schriftlich

(Verfassen einer englischsprachigen Tätigkeitsbeschreibung nach Stichworten)

★ The local newspaper in Fiona's new home town, The New Plymouth Herald, has asked her for an interview because they want to publish a feature story about German nurses in New Zealand. The journalist has asked her for a short job description in advance to prepare for the interview.

YOUR TASK Write a report "Typical activities of a registered nurse for the elderly" which is based on Fiona's notes.

My working life at Active Silver Life: typical activities of a registered nurse for the elderly

- physiotherapy
- dressing
- breathing exercises
- exercise therapy
- personal hygiene
- meals/eating
- skin care
- change of bandages
- medication
- irrigation
- injections
- putting the patient in another bed
- billing of care procedures
- writing reports
- first aid
- team meetings
- cooperation with doctors
- documentation of care procedures
- organising events and parties for the residents and their relatives
- helping the residents to establish a social net
- encouraging residents to talk
- contact with family members
- general encouragement
- giving advice

Teil 5 PRODUKTION eigene Stellungnahme

★ From time to time, Fiona checks the local and regional newspapers to see how New Plymouth Meadows Park and Active Silver Life are portrayed in New Zealand's press. In an article about aging Western societies, the journalist ends his comment with the following statement: "What this country and surely most Western societies need most of all are families who are willing and able to have their parents and grandparents stay with them for as long as possible. We should not press ahead with so-called retirement villages where hundreds of elderly citizens keep to themselves."

YOUR TASK Comment on the journalist's statement. Give reasons for your opinion.

Practice exam 3

★ Lioba Szesny, 22, lives and studies in Berlin. At present she is attending a three-year course in health management at Steglitzer Gesundheitswissenschaftsinstitut, an institute of applied sciences in health and social care. In order to finance her studies, Lioba has a part-time job working for one of her professors, Dr Marie Wilczek-Beul. At present they are preparing an international symposium on forms of teenage addiction to be held in Berlin. 60 scientists and health experts from all over the world have been invited to attend this conference.

A1.29 Teil 1 REZEPTION mündlich (Hörverstehen)

★ One of Lioba's tasks in preparing the conference is to set up an agenda for the two-day conference. This means that she has to organise the program, the seminars and of course the speakers. When she comes into her boss's office one morning, she finds the following message on Dr Wilczek-Beul's answerphone.

YOUR TASK Listen to the message and fill in the information on the message pad.

Anrufer ______________________________

Institut / Einrichtung ______________________________

Anlass ______________________________

____

____

____

____

____

Weitere Informationen ______________________________

____

____

____

____

____

Zu veranlassende Schritte ______________________________

____

____

____

____

____

____

Teil 2 MEDIATION

★ Professor Wilczek-Beul has given Lioba the following German text and has asked her to summarise its main parts in English as the introduction of her first paper at the conference.

YOUR TASK Work through the following German newspaper article and summarise its main parts in English.

Suchterkrankungen sind nach Expertenangaben eines der größten und teuersten Probleme moderner Gesellschaften; aktuelle Zahlen belegen, dass in Europa bereits mehr als 10% der im Gesundheitswesen aufgewendeten Kosten in die Behandlung unterschiedlicher Abhängigkeiten und deren Folgen fließen.
Sucht wird von der Weltgesundheitsorganisation WHO als ein Zustand chronischer oder periodischer Berauschung bezeichnet, wobei der als angenehm empfundene und in der Wiederholung angestrebte Bewusstseinszustand durch die Einnahme einer natürlichen oder synthetischen Droge erreicht wird.

Kritiker dieser offiziellen Definition führen an, dass Sucht im 21. Jahrhundert nicht immer nur mit Drogen, d.h. Substanzen, in Verbindung gebracht werden dürfe. Mit dem Vormarsch u.a. des Internets und der Zunahme des sozialen Wohlstands haben sich zahlreiche verhaltensabhängige Suchtformen entwickelt.
Dementsprechend wird in der Suchtforschung unterschieden zwischen substanzabhängigen und verhaltensbezogenen Suchtformen:

Bei den substanzabhängigen Suchtformen, die auch als stoffgebunden bezeichnet werden, gibt es zwei Untergruppen, die – je nach geltenden Bestimmungen – legalen und die illegalen Suchtstoffe. Während u.a. Alkohol, Tabak, Kaffee und Tabletten in einem gewissen Rahmen legal sind, werden beispielsweise Marihuana, Crack, LSD, Heroin und Haschisch als illegal eingestuft.
Anders als die substanzabhängigen Suchtformen wird bei Suchttätigkeiten Erfüllung und Befriedigung durch eine zwanghaft ausgeübte Tätigkeit erreicht. Zu diesen Tätigkeiten bzw. Süchten gehören z.B. Computer- und Fernsehkonsum, Spiel- und Kaufsucht, Ess- und Sexsucht etc.

Teil 3 REZEPTION Leseverstehen

★ A professor from the UK is going to lecture on mobile phone addiction. As Lioba has already been sent the scripts of many lectures, she studies the following text.

YOUR TASK Work through the following text and complete the diagram on page 70.

Most of us are becoming increasingly reliant on communication technology. Mobile phones, for example, are already more than just a phone. They are also used as alarm clocks, watches, music players, cameras, calendars, for the weather forecast or as a navigation device.
Recent surveys in which Americans named their cell phone a device they "can least go out without" stated two alarming facts:

1. Increasingly, mobile phones are reported to interfere with personal relationships, classroom lectures, productivity at work, and traffic safety all over the world.

2. A growing number call their cell phone "an essential item, an extension of self."

What is true for many mobile phone users in general becomes an alarming development when we look at teenagers and the amount of time they spend with their phone.
When asked how many hours a day she spends on her mobile, a blogger from the UK posted the following:
I spend every minute on my phone when I'm awake. So I would say 6–12 hours a day. When my phone goes off at night I answer it right away! My friends are the same: their phone is their world. Without it I don't know how I would function. I know this is bad but I gotta stay in touch with the world and that's the only way!

A study from the USA found that young people with excessive use of cell phones
- have a generally more careless lifestyle
- consume more stimulating beverages
- have difficulty in falling asleep and suffer from disrupted sleep
- are more susceptible to stress and fatigue

Scientists from all over the world who specialise in teenagers' use of mobile phones agree that the following symptoms might well constitute the beginning of an addiction:

Teenagers
- feel uncomfortable when they are not using a cell phone
- neglect the obligations of important activities (e.g. job or studies)
- show irrational reactions to being without a phone
- constantly check whether they have lost or fogotten their phone
- spend more and more time talking on a cell phone
- get higher mobile phone bills that cause financial distress
- have problems at school and work from constant cell phone use
- have interpersonal problems from constant cell phone use
- take unnecessary risks such as using a cell phone while driving

Some parents' organisations have come up with tips to limit their children's mobile phone use. Among other things they suggest:
- Set your child specific times during the day when he or she can use their cell phone.
- Only use prepaid cards to limit the money spent on phone calls.
- Encourage activities and hobbies where mobile phones are in the way (especially sports)
- Ask your child to turn off the cell phone at a certain time each evening.

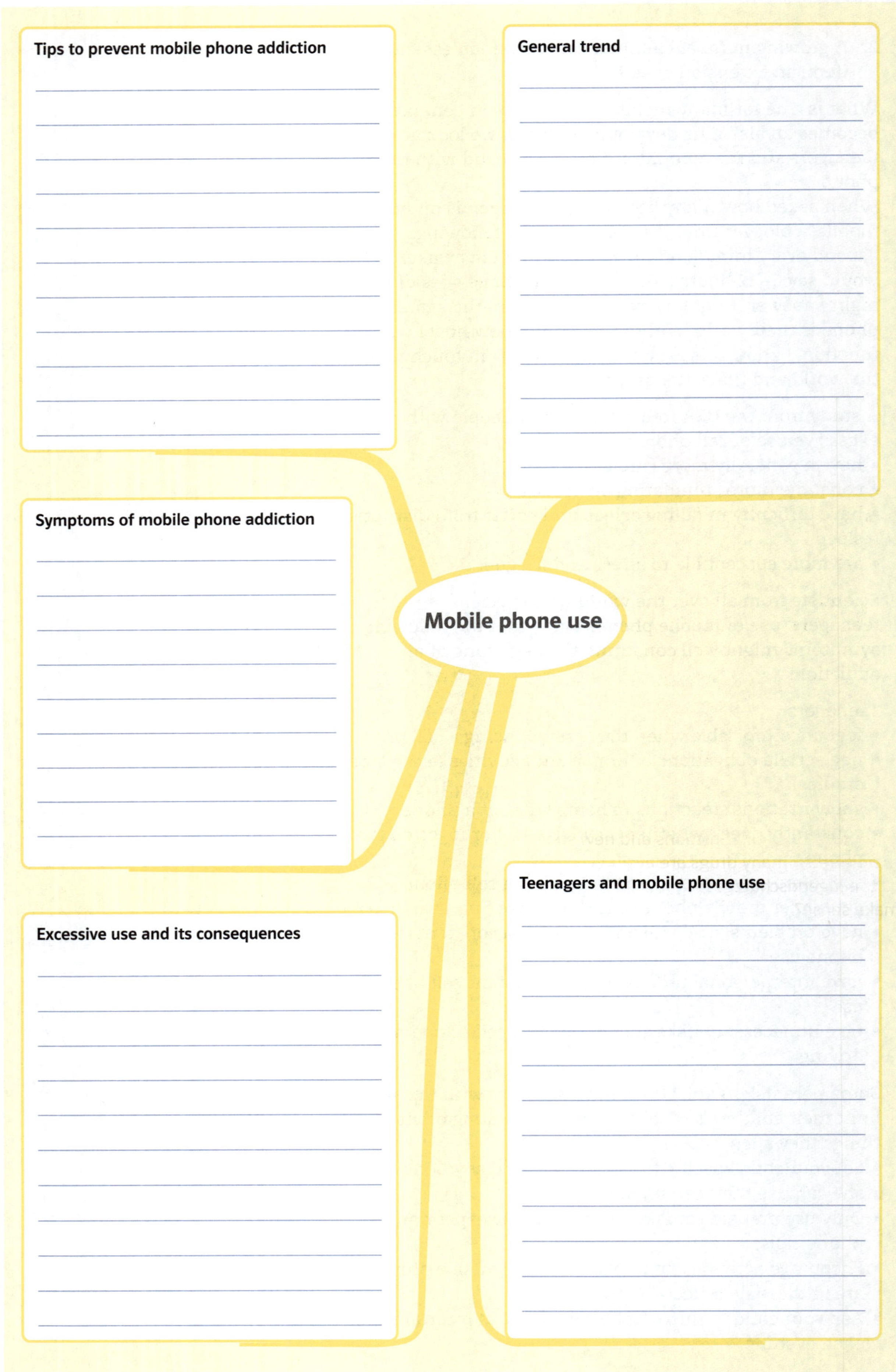
Tips to prevent mobile phone addiction
General trend
Symptoms of mobile phone addiction
Mobile phone use
Excessive use and its consequences
Teenagers and mobile phone use

Teil 4 PRODUKTION schriftlich

(Verfassen eines englischsprachigen Berichts nach Diagrammvorgaben)

★ Professor Wilczek-Beul asks Lioba to write a short English report about German children and teenagers who have to be treated in hospital due to excessive alcohol consumption. The text should be based on the diagram below.

YOUR TASK **Write Lioba's report.**

Stationäre Krankenhausaufenthalte von Kindern und Jugendlichen aufgrund akuter Alkoholintoxikation

Source: Statistisches Bundesamt Deutschland

Teil 5 PRODUKTION eigene Stellungnahme

★ If new forms of addictions and new substances are appearing rapidly and if many drugs are available nearly everywhere, do laws such as the Jugendschutzgesetz (law for the protection of the youth) still make sense?.

YOUR TASK **Comment on the question. Give reasons for your opinion.**

Bildquellennachweis

5 JupiterImages photos.com, Tucson, AZ; **5** iStockphoto (Lise Gagne), Calgary, Alberta; **6** iStockphoto (Rich Legg), Calgary, Alberta; **6** shutterstock (CURAphotography), New York, NY; **8** iStockphoto (Tyler Stalman), Calgary, Alberta; **12** iStockphoto (nullplus), Calgary, Alberta; **12** iStockphoto (michellegibson), Calgary, Alberta; **13** iStockphoto (daaronj), Calgary, Alberta; **14** iStockphoto (Jani Bryson), Calgary, Alberta; **18** iStockphoto (MorePixels), Calgary, Alberta; **19** iStockphoto (Silvrshootr), Calgary, Alberta; **21** iStockphoto (pamspix), Calgary, Alberta; **23** iStockphoto (Jacob Wackerhausen), Calgary, Alberta; **27** iStockphoto (Jeanell Norvell), Calgary, Alberta; **30** iStockphoto (Jordan Chesbrough), Calgary, Alberta; **31** iStockphoto (David Kneafsey), Calgary, Alberta; **36** shutterstock (Magdalena Bujak), New York, NY; **41** iStockphoto (digitalskillet), Calgary, Alberta; **44** iStockphoto (TommL), Calgary, Alberta; **44** iStockphoto (Sami Suni), Calgary, Alberta; **46** Avenue Images GmbH RF (Imgram Publishing), Hamburg; **50** iStockphoto (MissHibiscus), Calgary, Alberta; **51** Thinkstock (Hemera), München; **51** Thinkstock (Stockbyte), München; **54** iStockphoto (Petro Feketa), Calgary, Alberta; **56** Klett-Archiv (A. Raftaki), Stuttgart; **57** Thinkstock (iStockphoto), München; **COVER** shutterstock (Andrey Armyagov), New York, NY; **COVER** Jörg Lantelme, Kassel; **Lösungheft Titelbild** Jörg Lantelme, Kassel; **Lösungsheft Titelbild** shutterstock (Andrey Armyagov), New York, NY

Sollte es in einem Einzelfall nicht gelungen sein, den korrekten Rechteinhaber ausfindig zu machen, so werden berechtigte Ansprüche selbstverständlich im Rahmen der üblichen Regelungen abgegolten.

Lösungsheft zum Workbook

social & health EXPERT

Soziales & Gesundheit

Klett

Unit 1

1

1. *Ireland*
2. UK
3. Denmark
4. (the) Netherlands
5. Sweden
6. Finland
7. Estonia
8. Latvia
9. Lithuania
10. Poland
11. Germany
12. Belgium
13. Luxembourg
14. France
15. Portugal
16. Spain
17. Italy
18. Austria
19. Czech Republic
20. Slovakia
21. Hungary
22. Slovenia
23. Romania
24. Bulgaria
25. Cyprus
26. Greece
27. Malta

1 27
2 Turkey
3 Norway
4 Switzerland
5 (19)93
6 1951
7 travel
8 work
9 nationalities
10 euro
11 Eurozone
12 Britain / the UK

2

C eine zeitlich begrenzte Handlung in der Gegenwart
A Handlungen in der Gegenwart, die auf Dauer gültig sind
D Zukunftspläne
B Ereignisse in der Vergangenheit

3

1 *come*
2 live
3 wasn't born
4 lived
5 moved
6 was
7 went
8 left
9 'm studying
10 'm enjoying
11 want
12 'm going to work
13 visited
14 loved
15 plan
16 'd like / would like

4

1 *is*
2 is
3 works
4 likes
5 has
6 thinks
7 isn't
8 's doing
9 's spending
10 's training
11 is
12 'm learning
13 like
14 want

5

1 *do you come*
2 are you spending here?
3 What course are you doing? (...are you on?)
4 did you come here?
5 do you like the town?

6

Individuelle Lösungen

7

1 *o*; 2 h; 3 i; 4 j; 5 b; 6 a;
7 g; 8 d; 9 c; 10 n;
11 m; 12 k; 13 f; 14 e; 15 l

1. *law*
2. in favour of
3. currency
4. parliament
5. standard of living
6. War
7. alternative
8. unthinkable
9. mobile
10. democracy, right

8

a trading bloc
b consumer
c environment
d education system

Beispiellösungen
a With 500 million people, the EU is the world's biggest trading bloc.
b Food labelling helps consumers to know what is in a food product.
c We all want a clean and green environment.
d The education system in Germany is different from the education system in the UK.

9

1. *Finn, Finnish*
2. Pole, Polish
3. Portuguese
4. Belgians
5. Norwegians
6. Irishwoman
7. Bulgarian, Italian, Hungarian
8. Swiss
9. Spaniard
10. Icelandic
11. Turkish

Video lounge

1

1. *supposed*, my mind
2. baggage allowance
3. hang out with
4. easy reach
5. enrol
6. start ... scratch
7. together
8. pretty much
9. transition, readjusting
10. working on
11. something ... going on

2

Beispiellösungen
Section 1
1. Paris. She visited a friend in Berlin in November and came back for New Year. She (just) had a good feeling about Berlin.
2. Thousands of lakes and forests and places like Wannsee. Everyone decamps to the beach.
3. Three or four friends (from London). Extra baggage allowance.
4. She had no home, no job, and couldn't speak the language.

5. She got her bike, enrolled at a language school, found a place to live and is now working on finding a job.

Section 2

6. She started with some language books. She found the books in a box in the street in a part of London called Soho.
7. She's learning German. She has friends there and it gives her a social life.

Section 3

8. They were shocked and surprised that Seema didn't go to Paris (as expected). Later, they were 'cool'.
9. It's easy to move around. There are people from around the world in every city. There's a real European culture thing going on. Seema thinks young people should 'go out there, try it.'

3

Beispiellösung

Seema Prabhu is a 26-year-old English journalist who is living in Berlin at the moment. She came to Berlin after a couple of visits to the city because she liked it so much. Seema's life in Berlin was hard at first. She didn't speak German, and she didn't have a flat or a job. Now she is happy there. One important thing for her was enrolling at a language school. She learned German there and she also met lots of people. Seema's parents were surprised when she went to Berlin (she was supposed to go to Paris). But now they are 'cool' about it. Seema thinks that all young people should travel. She believes there's a 'European culture thing going on'.

(121 words)

Unit 2

1

1 i; 2 m; 3 h; 4 g; 5 b; 6 j; 7 n; 8 l; 9 a; 10 e; 11 c; 12 f; 13 d; 14 k; 15 p; 16 o; 17 r; 18 q; 19 t; 20 s

2

Jane Wilkins	Gerrit Mühlkamp
Do you mind if I join you? (5b)	No, not at all, take a seat. (13d)
So are you enjoying the party so far? (2m)	Yes, I do. The food is nice, the people are friendly and I like the music. (9a)
By the way, I'm Jane, Jane Wilkins. (7n)	Pleased to meet you, Jane, my name's Gerrit, Gerrit Mühlkamp. (6j)
Where do you come from? Are you Swedish? (14k)	No, actually I'm German. I'm from Braunschweig, that's in Lower Saxony. (11c)
So what are you doing here in Norwich, Gerrit? (12f)	I'm here on a trainee programme for six months. (3h)
I see. Which job do you do and which company do you work for? (8l)	I am training to become a dietician and work for the German food producer Goldbrecht. They mainly make convenience food such as pizza, lasagne etc. (4g)
And how then did you end up here in Norwich? (1i)	Goldbrecht and the Norwich based company Nourwell Ltd are business partners. They have agreed on a mutual trainee programme. (10e)
I see. That means that someone from Norwich is now staying in Braunschweig with your company? (16o)	Exactly, we have more or less swapped our workplaces for half a year. (15p)
Is this your first visit to the UK? (17r)	No, I was in London with my parents when I was 10 or 11. But I have to admit that I do not remember that much. (18q) What about you? Have you ever been to Germany? (19t)
No, I have to admit that I haven't. But I spent a week in Zurich two years ago. (20s)	...

3

Beispiellösungen

1. TALKING ABOUT YOUR HOBBIES AND INTERESTS
   free time, leisure, I like ..., my hobbies are ...:
   meeting friends, sports, listening to music, computer games, shopping

2. WHERE YOU LIVE
   a small town, a large town, a village, inhabitants, north/south/east/west of Germany, ... kilometres away from ..., (not) much to do in your free time

3. FUTURE PLANS
   work abroad for some time, have a good job, maybe a family, enough free time, live in a larger city

4

Individuelle Lösungen

Unit 3

1

1. *parent* does not fit – you normally meet the other persons at school every day
2. *pupil* does not fit – the other three are adults
3. *music teacher* does not fit – the other three do not teach
4. *nurse* does not fit – the other three teach
5. *parents rep* does not fit – the other three get paid for their work
6. *to oversee* does not fit – the other three have to do with learning, *to oversee* just means controlling
7. *afternoon* does not fit – the other three are activities or organised time at school
8. *administration* does not fit – the other three begin with the letter „t", and they are -ing-forms of verbs describing activities
9. *bus* does not fit – the other three are rooms in a school

2

1 c; 2 e; 3 f; 4 b; 5 a; 6 d; 7 h; 8 i; 9 g

3

Beispiellösungen
1. find a partner school
3. introduce your school
5. inform pupils and parents
7. visit your partner school
8. receive visitors from partner school

4

1 d; 2 c; 3 b; 4 e; 5 g; 6 h; 7 a; 8 f

(andere Lösungen sind möglich)

5

1. Last year, the school started an exchange programme with a German school in Cologne.
2. In 2009, the school won an award for their healthy school meal.
3. There are a playground and a playing field next to the gym.
4. The school is very proud of its very efficient cooperation with the parents.

6

Individuelle Lösungen

Video lounge

1

Individuelle Lösungen

2

general information
- private school
- financed by school fees (£1,500/year)
- founded 25 years ago
- no government control

experiment
started 25 years ago

difference
In some schools pupils like what they do, here the pupils do what they like; no bells, no homework, no exams.

taking classes
- pupils decide if they want to take a class
- many pupils are not taking any classes

lessons
- no regular lessons
- pupils go to a teacher and ask for a class

what to learn
- pupils decide what they want to learn
- they ask a teacher for a lesson
- when the pupils are not taking any classes they learn how to socialise

how to learn
- idea: children know what is best for them, they only learn if they want to, if you learn because you want to you will remember easily
- pupils from different age groups learn together
- you learn by talking to people

rules
- nobody tells you what to do
- rules are made by pupils

decisions
- pupils choose for themselves how to spend their day
- weekly meetings: pupils decide about the running of the school, about the employment of teachers etc.

teachers
- teachers give lessons when they are asked to
- they are hired and fired by the pupils

3

Individuelle Lösungen

Unit 4

1

1. *mike.harris@google.com*
2. l.williams@bt-online.co.uk
3. ina.krueger@web.de
4. liv.wagner@markert_sales.de
5. bodo-richter@koeln_net.de

2

1. *Would you please send me the dates of the health fair next month?*
2. Would / Could you please email me the name of your new assistant?
3. Would / Could you please let me have the telephone number of your Irish office?
4. *Could you tell me / let me know when you will send your report?*
5. Could you tell me / let me know where your distribution offices in the Netherlands are?
6. Could you tell me / let me know if you have Ms Jones's mobile number?
7. Would / Could you please email me the dates when your office will be closed?
8. Could you tell me / let me know if someone will meet me at the airport?
9. Could you tell me / let me know where the new dental laboratory is?
10. Would / Could you please let us have your decision asap?

3

1. Melissa Taylor (24 October 17.15) wants some sales literature. Melissa again (24 October 17.18) wants the dates of Ms Dabbert's next visit to the UK.
2. Rafael Costa is sending you details of the health fair in Madrid. Wim de Vries is letting you know the Amsterdam office will be closed on 28 and 29 November.

4

Rafael
1 the health fair in Madrid next month.
2 Could you please send
3 in advance

Beispiellösungen

Melissa (E-Mail 1)
Dear Melissa
Thanks for your email. We're also excited about the product launch. Sales brochures will be available on 15 November. We'll send them to you immediately by post.
Best regards

Melissa (E-Mail 2)
Hello again Melissa
I'm attaching the details of Ms Dabbert's next trip. We can book hotels here, but would you please organise / arrange for a hire car? Thanks!
With best wishes

Wim
Thank you for the information.
Please let us know if you will be contactable / if we will be able to contact you by phone on the 28th and 29th. Do you have a mobile number for us?
Would you also please send us your monthly failure rates for November by 27 November?
Good luck with the move / reorganisation.
All the best

5

1. *in*
2. attachment
3. let
4. forward
5. wanted
6. asked
7. further
8. sorry
9. afraid
10. open
11. things
12. Fine
13. attaching
14. Could / Would

Unit 5

1

ACROSS
2 nursing assistant
6 care
7 injection
8 night shift
9 message
10 elderly
13 resident
14 doctor
15 administration
16 janitor

DOWN
1 retirement home
3 routine
4 pharmaceutical
5 visitor
11 decorations
12 medication

2

Individuelle Lösungen

3

social contacts
- regular walks around your neighbourhood or the local park
- network of friends
- get involved in different social groups
- use the internet to keep in contact with friends who live far away

mental fitness
- crossword puzzles
- game that requires a lot of thinking
- read books

physical fitness and nutrition
- get enough exercise and eat a lot of healthy food
- regular walks
- regular physical exercise

medical issues
- see your doctor regularly
- early diagnosis might cure illness
- know about possible side effects of your medication

your attitude
- accept that you are getting older
- actively fight problems that might come up
- do not get stressed

4

Individuelle Lösungen

5

Individuelle Lösungen

6

	VERB	NOUN
1	to care	care
2	to retire	retirement
3	to decorate	decoration
4	to arrange	arrangement
5	to deliver	delivery
6	to chat	chat
7	to arrive	arrival
8	to sign	signature
9	to repair	repair
10	to access	access
11	to require	requirements
12	to decide	decision
13	to plan	plan
14	to choose	choice
15	to assist	assistance
16	to transport	transport
17	to lift	lift
18	to visit	visit
19	to promise	promise

7

Individuelle Lösungen

Unit 6

1

1 bereavement
2 patients
3 cope
4 death
5 Grief
6 loss
7 professional
8 detached
9 strongly
10 condolence
11 member
12 affected
13 pain
14 behaviour
15 emotions
16 challenges
17 staff

2

1. to deal with something
2. to grieve
3. loss
4. to feel strongly
5. relative
6. to express how strongly you feel
7. condolence

3

Individuelle Lösungen

Unit 7

1

ACROSS
1 harmful
3 difficulty
6 restrict
10 harm
11 online
14 symptoms
15 inevitable
16 prohibit
19 addict
21 entertainment
22 spend
23 need
24 tobacco

DOWN
2 addiction
4 crime
5 violence
7 treatment
8 values
9 gambling
12 passive smoking
13 TV
17 recognize
18 internet
20 relax

2

Individuelle Lösungen

3

1. *large (adj.)*
2. famous (adj.)
3. easily (adv.)
4. quickly (adv.)
5. interesting (adj.)
6. amazing (adj.)
7. excellent (adj.)
8. interested (adj.)
9. careful (adj.)
10. carefully (adv.)
11. automatic (adj.)
12. automatically (adv.)
13. extremely (adv.)
14. amazingly (adv.)
15. totally (adv.)
16. incredibly (adv.)

4

Individuelle Lösungen

5

1. *bad* does not fit - the other terms describe a negative effect on one's health
2. *TV* does not fit – the other three stand for substances which are forbidden for children
3. *stealing* does not fit – it is against the law
4. *help* does not fit – the other three stand for organised professional assistance
5. *resident* does not fit – the other three stand for someone who needs professional assistance
6. *fulfilment* does not fit – it describes an effect you try to achieve with the help of the other terms
7. *patient* does not fit – the other three are used in the context of alcohol addiction
8. *foreign* does not fit – it means coming from somewhere else
9. *hesitant* does not fit – the other three describe an unwillingness to do something
10. *forbidden* does not fit – the other terms stand for something which is against the law
11. *restlessness* does not fit – the other terms describe a state of being afraid

6

Individuelle Lösungen

Video lounge

1

a 3; b 6; c 7; d 2; e 1; f 4; g 5

2

Individuelle Lösungen

3

Beispiellösung
In den Innenstädten Großbritanniens gibt es eine wachsende Zahl von jungen Menschen (hauptsächlich zwischen 18 und 24 Jahre alt), die als *binge drinkers* bezeichnet werden. *Binge drinking* bezeichnet den Konsum von mehr als 4 Pint Bier oder einer Flasche Wein an einem Abend.

Fast die Hälfte der Männer und ein Viertel der Frauen werden als *binge drinkers* bezeichnet. Dies hat sowohl negative finanzielle wie auch gesundheitliche Auswirkungen. Die Regierung sieht die Gefahr einer Kultur des Rausches, die die Gesellschaft bedrohe, und möchte eine Wende zu einer Trinkkultur im Stil von Cafè-Besuchen. Dies würde vor allem ältere Menschen wieder in die Innenstädte bringen, was einen mäßigenden Einfluss auf das Verhalten der jungen Menschen haben könnte.

Unit 8

1

1 j; 2 k; 3 g; 4 l; 5 i; 6 e; 7 b; 8 a; 9 c; 10 d;
11 f; 12 h

2

1 spend
2 colleagues
3 co-workers
4 co-operation
5 relationship
6 performance
7 respect
8 attitude
9 criticism
10 object
11 makes
12 useful
13 gossip
14 atmosphere
15 waste
16 extra-work
17 competitors

3

My ideal workplace
This is what my ideal workplace would look like:
The general atmosphere in the company or organisation is friendly and relaxed, you can say that there is respect for everyone. Even when problems or questions arise which might take some time to be solved you always get help and assistance.
Your performance on the job is what really counts. This is also the most important aspect in the management's decision on who gets a job and who gets promoted.
Handicapped co-workers are not seen as costly staff but as valuable colleagues who have their own qualifications and ideas.
My ideal workplace has got a canteen where the food is both free and very good.
There are no fixed times when you need to be in. Whenever you have finished your work you may go home. Furthermore, it doesn't matter if you work from the office or from home.
The pay in general is good, you do not feel that you are not getting anything in return for the work you invest. Of course there always is a fair chance to get promoted, too.
You do not have to argue with your colleagues about your holidays.
Your superiors and the management in general know what they are talking about. They know who is doing a good job; they are fair and give positive feedback.

4

Individuelle Lösungen

Unit 9

1

Individuelle Lösungen

2

The diagram shows a comparison of registered offences in three age groups (14- to 18-year olds, 18- to 21-year olds, 21+). The registered offences do not include traffic-related offences.
The group of teenagers aged 14-18 have two large categories which account for nearly 50% of the offences: assault and vandalism/theft. A third category (aggravated theft, robbery, blackmail) is significant as well and accounts for nearly 20% of the offences in this age group. Drug offences do not play an important role.
The age group of adolescents (18-21) commit more crimes which can be summarised by the term fraud. Theft still accounts for nearly 20% of the crimes. Most drug offences are registered in this age group.
When looking at the age group of adults we see the highest number of crimes in the category fraud offences. Vandalism and theft account for approximately 20% of the offences, drug offences and assaults are less significant.
All in all it can be said that the older the people get the higher the number of fraud offences are. Other crimes such as assault, (aggravated) theft, robbery and blackmail become less important. Drug offences are most significant in the group of 18- to 21-year olds.

3

1. Crime as such cannot be measured.
2. Crime statistics only show what the police and the state deal with.
3. Statistics cannot show the number of actual illegal actions.
4. Police and public prosecution can only act when a crime has officially been reported.
5. If statistics say that today there are more cases of assault, this can also mean that today more victims dare talk to the police.
6. Statistics change, so do the societies in which crimes are committed. This cannot be shown in statistics.
7. International statistics do not show that in different countries different crimes are regarded as illegal. If for example, the consumption of cannabis is illegal in only some countries, then comparisons are not possible.

4

Individuelle Lösungen

5

Individuelle Lösungen

Video lounge

1

arguments against CCTV
- only few people are convicted as a result of CCTV
- criminals take their crimes to other places

views of the general public
- CCTV reassures the general public
- makes people less fearful of crime
- local businesses: shoppers feel safer with CCTV
- CCTV reduces crime
- cameras could be an infringement of civil liberties
- criminals are more likely to get caught

efficiency of CCTV
- in Sutton crime fell by a fifth in the shopping area and by 93% in nearby car parks
- pubs and shops with no CCTV: increase in crimes (handbag thefts)
- few people are convicted as a result of CCTV
- criminals take their crimes to places with no CCTV

reasons for installing CCTV
- vehicles left in car parks are being vandalised or stolen
- staff cars are broken into
- stolen radio
- cars are stolen, or parts of the car are taken (badges, bumpers)

how it works
- a crime is watched by CCTV cameras
- the control room alerts a security guard
- the guard chases the criminal

2

Individuelle Lösungen

3

Beispiellösung
After watching the video about CCTV systems in Great Britain the question arises if this system of camera control should be installed in Germany as well. Whenever public discussions about crime rates in Germany arise, many people immediately ask for technical devices which should make the public feel safer.

Of course, many people feel that especially in city centres crime rates are far too high. They say that CCTV cameras could prevent illegal activities because criminals fear they might get caught easily. This should especially go for theft, robbery and drug trafficking. Another argument is that we already have these camera systems in operation in some places where providing the feeling of security seems very important, e.g. in underground stations, at cash dispensers, motorway tunnels etc. Furthermore, supporters of this system add that just the fact that these cameras are very visible in the city centres will have a positive effect: shoppers will feel much safer, criminals will feel watched.

On the other hand there are various arguments which speak against these systems. First of all there is the question of efficiency. If we look at those countries which already use CCTV in their cities, their reports are not really stories of success. Rather than reducing crime, crime rates grow dramatically in areas where there is no TV surveillance. Then there is the question of costs. These systems need to be installed and maintained, there has to be staff (presumably the police) who constantly watch the monitors to trace illegal activity.
Last but not least the question of personal freedom arises. If the authorities are allowed to track all our movements in cities, where does this kind of state control stop? How can we be sure that the data are not stored, analysed and sold to whoever might be interested?

When looking at the arguments for and against CCTV cameras I believe that we should restrict the use of these surveillance systems to places where there seems to be a need for increased security, i.e. at cash dispensers, in underground stations or for traffic control.

Unit 10

1

1 g / j / k; 2 j / k / l; 3 j / k / l; 4 h; 5 e / f / g; 6 a; 7 b / h; 8 e / f / g; 9 c; 10 k; 11 i; 12 d

2

Beispiellösungen
a Would you like me to spell my name?
b Could you please give me your name and the name of your company?
c Can I just repeat the message you would like me to give to …
d Can I just check if I understood that correctly?
e Would you like to leave a message?
f Can I give you my boss's mobile number so that you can phone him right away?
g Would you mind giving me your mobile number?
h Could you please repeat you name?
i Would you please tell me the number of … in …

3

1 *This is*
2 message
3 received
4 survey
5 to receiving
6 treatment
7 invite
8 details
9 post
10 accommodation
11 conference
12 contact
13 give me
14 out of
15 incoming
16 to hearing

4

1 c; 2 c; 3 a; 4 c; 5 c; 6 b; 7 a; 8 c; 9 a; 10 c

5

2. Pankratius
   Papa – Alfa – November – Kilo – Romeo – Alfa – Tango – India – Uniform – Sierra
3. Braunschweig
   Bravo – Romeo – Alfa – Uniform – November – Sierra – Charlie – Hotel – Whisky – Echo – India – Golf
4. Zimmermann
   Zulu – India – Mike – Mike – Echo – Romeo – Mike – Alfa – November – November
5. Seniorenstift
   Sierra – Echo – November – India – Oscar – Romeo – Echo – November – Sierra – Tango – India – Foxtrot – Tango
6. Kleinberger
   Kilo – Lima – Echo – India – November – Bravo – Echo – Romeo – Golf – Echo – Romeo
7. Michalsky
   Mike – India – Charlie – Hotel – Alfa – Lima – Sierra – Kilo – Yankee
8. Annegret
   Alfa – November – November – Echo – Golf – Romeo – Echo – Tango

6

1.

To	Mrs Jürgenbauer
Date	...
Time	...
Caller	Liv Ulmansson
Company	Swedish Medical Association
Phone number	0046-77-6923-345
Message	Ms Ulmansson will be arriving a day late at the Zurich conference, she would like to postpone the meeting due to urgent matters. She hopes that next Wednesday (17th) is suitable.
Taken by	(name)

2.

To	Mr Wimmer
Date	...
Time	...
Caller	Margareta Halvorsen
Company	Stockholm University
Phone number	0046-8-10 13 66
Message	Ms Halvorsen has been given final approval for European nutrition research programme; everything can go ahead as planned, meeting in Sweden next month. She would like to have some dates when you're free to arrange the meeting.
Taken by	(name)

7

Beispiellösung

A: Gleiswitz, Pankratius Grundschule. Was kann ich für Sie tun?
B: This is Stuart Peterson, deputy head of St Margaret's Primary School in York. Do you speak English?
A: Yes, I do. What can I do for you, Mr Peterson?
B: We are planning an exchange programme for our pupils and now we are looking for a partner school in the south of Germany. I saw your homepage on the internet and would like to get to know you and your school if that is at all possible.
A: Of course, Mr Peterson, I am pleased to hear that you liked our homepage. Basically, we are interested in a school exchange as we have been teaching English for two years now. When would you like to start your exchange?
B: If possible, we would like to visit you with our first group in July next year; you – or whichever German school – would come over to York in September.
A: That sounds fine to me. But I need to talk to my colleagues and the parents rep about this idea first. You will surely understand that.
B: Of course I do. In the meantime could you do us a favour and send us a short description of your school in English? Of course we will let you have a description of our school, too.
A: Yes, no problem. When do you suggest should we get in touch again? I could give you a call once I have talked to my colleagues and the parents rep.
B: That sounds fine, when would that be?
A: Within two weeks at the latest. Could you please give me your phone number?
B: Sure, that's 0044, country code for Great Britain, then 1904, area code, and the local number is 843 283. My email is S.peterson@margaretprimary.co.uk
A: Just a second please, could you please spell that for me?
B: Of course, that's S DOT P – E – T – E – R – S – O – N AT M – A – R – G – A – R – E – T – P – R – I – M – A – R – Y DOT C – O DOT U – K. Could I have your email as well, please?
A: Of course, it's Gleiswitz@gs-pankratius.de.
B: Thank you ever so much. I am looking forward to hearing from you again soon.
A: Thank you, talk to you again soon. Bye!
B: Bye!

8

Individuelle Lösungen

Unit 11

1

ACROSS		DOWN	
3	found	1	adoption
6	decade	2	teenager
7	abortion	4	divorce
9	contraceptive	5	parents
11	marry	8	relationship
12	pregnant	10	traditional
15	adopt	13	marriage
16	polygamy	14	counselling
17	stepfather	18	prenatal
21	education	19	family
22	HIV	20	single parent
23	legal	25	generation
24	pregnancy		
26	cohabitation		

2

1. growth, freedom
2. patterns, decades
3. same-sex
4. single
5. delay
6. developments
7. rise, cohabitation
8. divorces
9. households
10. values, generation
11. traditional, concept

Order:
11 – 6 – 2 – 4 – 3 – 5 – 7 – 8 – 9 – 1 – 10

3

The diagram shows marital status and children of women in two age groups. The first age group consists of women who in 2006 were between 50 and 75 years old, the second age group includes women who were between 30 and 49 when the survey was carried out. For each age group there are two sub-categories: children and no children.

In the older age group more than 80% of the women who have children are married or widows, under 10% are divorced, just a very small fraction is single. In that age group the percentage of single women among those women without children is quite high (35%). The number of those who do not have children and are divorced is small (just over 5%). When summarising the facts for this age group it can be said that having children usually goes along with being married.

The younger age group again has the categories children and no children. The group of those who are married with children is as significant as in the older age group (nearly 80%). Just the number of those who are single and have children is considerably higher (approx. 10%). When looking at those in the younger age group who have no children we can see major differences. The largest proportion in that age group and category are those who are single. When summarising the facts for this age group we can say that the number of those who are not married – no matter if they have children or not – are higher than in the age group of those who are between 50 and 75.

4

The main task of adoption agencies is to find the most suitable parents for a child needing a new family. Basically adoption agencies check two things: First of all they have a look at the facts, then they carry out a thorough examination to see if the parents will cope with being adoptive parents. They ask the following questions and consider the following aspects:
Can the applicants meet the child's specific needs?
What can be said about the child's development?
What kind of life has the child lived so far?
What can be said about the adoptive parents' age, character, living circumstances, their ability to bring up and educate children? What is their social standing?
The adoption agency needs to check documents such as the family register as well.
If the applicants seem to be qualified as adoptive parents, the adoption agency will approve of their application. However, before the actual adoption can take place, there is a period called adoptive care. Here the adoption agencies can monitor the development and see if a parent-child relationship is developing. If that is the case, the adoption can finally take place.

Unit 12

2

Individuelle Lösungen

3

Individuelle Lösungen

4

- Der NHS ist mit 1,3 Millionen Beschäftigten einer der weltweit größten Arbeitgeber.
- In 1.600 Krankenhäusern, 29.000 Arztpraxen und 18.000 Zahnarztpraxen gibt es pro Tag mehr als 1,5 Millionen Patientenkontakte.
- Fast 80% der Beschäftigten sind weiblich, 30% sind Krankenschwestern.
- Die Grundüberzeugung für den NHS ist, dass eine gute Gesundheitsversorgung für alle – unabhängig vom finanziellen Status – zur Verfügung stehen sollte.
- Pro Woche behandelt jeder vollzeitbeschäftigte Arzt in den Arztpraxen im Schnitt 255 Patienten, die NHS Krankenwagen fahren zu mehr als 50,000 Einsätzen pro Woche.
- NHS Direct – die telefonische Gesundheitsberatung – nimmt am Tag mehr als 26.000 Telefonate an, was sich auf mehr als 9 Millionen Anrufe im Jahr addiert.

Unit 13

1

Individuelle Lösungen

2

1. *writer* does not fit – the other terms are used for somebody working for a newspaper
2. *brochure* does not fit – it describes a form in which texts are published
3. *inform* does not fit – it is used for giving neutral information
4. *website* does not fit – it describes digital information, the other terms are print media
5. *magazine* does not fit – it belongs to print media
6. *celebrity* does not fit – the other terms describe someone who is paid by a newspaper
7. *new* does not fit – the other terms are used for judging
8. *censor* does not fit – it is used for the control of the media

3

Individuelle Lösungen

4

1. Muriel said that cosmetic surgery was no longer reserved for celebrities. The procedures were now much more affordable and available than in the past.
2. She said that over the last decade prices for even the most complicated surgery had dropped.
3. Muriel told the listeners that another factor adding to the popularity of cosmetic surgery was that most procedures were now much safer and quicker.
4. Moreover she mentioned that people aged 35-50 had the most procedures. She said that this target group normally had the financial means to pay for the surgery.
5. She mentioned that references from former patients and open-house events were the best way to find customers. She added that these advertising campaigns were also much less costly.
6. Muriel informed her audience that experts agreed that it was very important to inform the patients about possible side effects of plastic surgery. A website with links to all kinds of documentation was an inexpensive way to reach the clinics' target groups, she said.
7. In addition she reported that critics argued that people needed to accept the way they looked. The critics said that buying plastic surgery like buying household appliances was a dangerous trend.
8. Muriel informed the listeners that reports said that especially teenagers were very much in danger of regarding their bodies as a collection of spare parts.
9. She added that this trend would in the long run ruin the good image plastic surgery had been able to create in recent years.
10. Muriel concluded that advertising and marketing campaigns should therefore focus on health aspects and factual information.

5

Individuelle Lösungen

Video lounge

2

a 1; b 3; c 8; d 5; e 7; f 6; g 2; h 4

3

Individuelle Lösungen

4

Beispiellösung
Berechnungen und Vorhersagen des Hadley Centre for Climate Prediction sagen eine gravierende Änderung des Massentourismus für Europa voraus. Bis zum Jahr 2050 wird es rund ums Mittelmeer zu heiß für Tourismus sein, stattdessen werden Millionen Urlauber auf der Suche nach garantiert warmen Wetter auch nach Großbritannien kommen. Diese Entwicklung im Zuge der globalen Erderwärmung würde das traditionelle Bild der britischen Küste gravierend ändern, schon jetzt bedeute allein diese Vorstellung viel Druck und Nervosität für die Anwohner. Natürlich sieht man in Gegenden wie Cornwall die überlebenswichtige Funktion von Tourismus, aber wenn ständig so viele Urlauber kämen wie im Augenblick zu den Schulferien, würde das das Verkehrsnetz, das Gesundheitssystem und die Wasserversorgung über Gebühr belasten. Die im Zuge des Massentourismus entstehenden Neubauten würden die Küstenregion in Großbritannien stark bedrohen.

Unit 14

1

ACROSS
1 accommodation
3 volunteers
4 poverty
7 challenge
9 conservation
15 developing countries
16 topic
17 support
18 provide
19 work permit

DOWN
2 development organisation
5 valuable
6 experience
8 strengths
9 charity
10 abroad
11 raise funds
12 skills
13 medical check
14 voluntary work

2

permit	*to permit*	*verb*
guidance	*to guide*	*verb*
to contribute	contribution	noun

to apply	application	noun
valuable	value	noun
experience	experience	noun
to check	check	noun
to volunteer	volunteer	noun
poverty	poor	adjective
to fight	fight	noun
developing	development	noun
capability	capable	adjective
awareness	aware	adjective
restoration	to restore	verb
organisation	to organise	verb
education	to educate	verb
applicant	to apply	verb
to decide	decision	noun
to renovate	renovation	noun
repair	to repair	verb

3

Individuelle Lösungen

Unit 15

1

Jedes Jahr geben Millionen Menschen Milliarden aus, um Gewicht zu verlieren und ihre Idealfigur zu bekommen. Häufig sind schnell Enttäuschungen da, wenn die neue Diät keine Wunder wirkt.
Das Geheimnis beim Gewichtsverlust ist so simpel wie logisch: Man muss sich gesund ernähren und sich bewegen, das heißt auch, mehr Kalorien verbrennen als man aufnimmt.
Die Tipps zum Gewichtsverlust lassen sich wie folgt zusammenfassen:
Die Ziele sollten realistisch sein. Frühstück ist die wichtigste Mahlzeit am Tag. Trotz Diät sollten Sie jeden Tag eine vernünftige Mahlzeit zu sich nehmen. Essen Sie langsam und hören Sie auf die Signale, die Ihnen Ihr Magen gibt. Trinken Sie viel Wasser. Ersetzen Sie Wasser nicht durch zucker- und kalorienreiche Getränke wie Cola oder Säfte. Auch Kaffee ist in Mengen nicht gut, da er dehydriert. Essen Sie nicht, weil Sie sich langweilen. Treiben Sie dann besser Sport. Walken oder joggen Sie jeden Tag. Seien Sie aber nicht frustriert, wenn Sie nicht sofort 8–10 Kilometer ohne Pause laufen können. Laufen Sie mit Partner oder Hund, dann macht es mehr Spaß.

2

Individuelle Lösungen

3

Individuelle Lösungen

Video Lounge

1

Individuelle Lösungen

2

Young people and STIs
- want to have fun, this means sex as well
- do not know much about STIs

STIs: facts and consequences
- sharp rise in STIs, figures increased up to 30% in recent years
- infections can lead to infertility, blindness, death

Going abroad: travel and STIs
- study showed holiday makers in Tenerife: 1/3 have sex with a new partner on holiday, 2/3 of these did not use a condom

Medical services in the UK
- can take two weeks to see a doctor about sexually transmitted infections
- service is overwhelmed, not everything can be covered

Government action
- spend millions to improve services

3

Dear Jessica,
I just watched a short film clip about sexually transmitted infections, STIs. In this film you said that you didn't really know much about these diseases. I am not a medical expert either, but we are discussing this in school at the moment so that I can tell you what I know.
Of course, being a teenager today means wanting to have fun, for many this means sex as well. Sadly, many people (adults as well!) know that sexually transmitted diseases exist but still do not use a condom when sleeping with someone they do not know.
I do not want to sound too preachy since I do not know you, but let me tell you that these infections really are dangerous. They can lead to infertility and even death.
I believe the safest way to protect yourself is to use a condom if you want to have sex. Condoms are cheap, easy to get and can be carried around wherever you go. Maybe you give this a thought, it might be worth it.
Regards

Unit 16

1

Land / Stadt	*Großbritannien/London*
Art des Unternehmens	Kindergarten, bilingual, Kinder zwischen 3 und 5 Jahren
Art der Tätigkeit(en)	Erzieherin
Voraussetzungen	gute Deutsch- und Englischkenntnisse, 18 Jahre alt, guter Teamplayer
Bezahlung	240 Pfund/Monat, freies Frühstück und Mittagessen
Unterkunft	GES Einrichtung hilft bei Suche nach Unterkunft
Name der Kontaktperson	Moira Sutcliffe

2

1 Walkenweg 17
33605 Bielefeld
Germany
2 Ms Moira Sutcliffe
GES Kindergarten London Ltd
Old Street 22
EC1 9JH London, UK
3 Dear Ms Sutcliffe
4 Application for internship advertised in Life Abroad
5 Life Abroad
6 a two-year full-time Health and Social Science course
7 Bielefeld
8 a nursery nurse once I have finished my degrees
9 a 4-week work placement last year
10 ice skating
11 Yours sincerely
12 Encl.: CV

3

1. *Dear Mr MacKenzie*
2. I would like to apply for the work placement which you advertised on the Canada Tourism website.
3. I am currently in the second year of a two-year course at a vocational college in Cologne, Germany.
4. As you will see from my CV, I have good English and computer skills.
5. I am hard working, keen to learn, and a good communicator.
6. I have previous work experience in the hotel industry. Last year in my summer holidays I worked in an international hotel in Turkey.
7. My interests include sport, music and dance (dancing).
8. I would very much welcome the opportunity to work in a Canadian hotel.
9. I hope that you will consider my application and I look forward to hearing from you.
10. Yours sincerely

4

Land / Stadt	Sri Lanka / Marawila
Art des Unternehmens	Give Hope Ltd, Betreiber von Kinderheimen in Sri Lanka
Art der Tätigkeit(en)	Praktikanten für Englischunterricht, Spiele mit Kindern, Internetblog
Voraussetzungen	gute Englischkenntnisse, Computerkenntnisse, Erfahrung im Umgang mit Kindern dieser Altersgruppe, Zuneigung und Einfühlungsvermögen, Geduld und Verständnis, Mindestalter 18
Bezahlung	320 Euro im Monat
Unterkunft	Unterbringung im Doppelzimmer
Name der Kontaktperson	info@givehope.org

E-Mail: Individuelle Lösungen

5

1. *to apply*, application
2. applicant
3. internship
4. advertisement
5. advertised
6. currently
7. hard working, keen to learn, reliable, a good communicator
8. A good knowledge of English
9. unpaid, wage

Practice Exam 1

Teil 1 Rezeption (Hörverstehen)

Hörtext, Track A 1.27

Good morning, Esther, this is Nancy Erlbaum speaking from CCC in Grand Rapids. CCC is the Ciderwood Community Center here in Grand Rapids and I'm the center manager. Esther, yesterday I got a call from your uncle asking whether we could offer you an internship for six months. Now I'm just phoning to say that we'd love to have you – there's always a lot to do here in our community center.

I'll send you some more details about the work we do by email later today. Just some information for the time being: CCC is a community center, which means that we offer all kinds of services and advice to the people in the Ciderwood area. At present our focus is on childcare, educational programmes which help people to prepare for job interviews or improve their computing skills etc, and also health-related courses such as healthy eating on a small budget, proper nutrition etc.

There are 17 people on the team here, and the atmosphere is just great. Most of us love our work. The center is open 6 days a week from 7 am till 8 pm.

If I understood your uncle correctly, you will be here from October 1 to March 31. Your uncle will provide you with accommodation in his home. I'm afraid we cannot offer you much in terms of pay; $85 a week is as much as you can expect but this should cover your travel and food expenses. You could email me to let me know whether you are interested in joining us. My email is Nancy.Erlbaum@ccc-grandrapids.org.

Well, I hope to hear from you soon!
Bye for now.

Caller's name Nancy Erlbaum, center manager at CCC Grand Rapids
Institution Ciderwood Community Center in Grand Rapids
Reason for calling Nancy is calling to offer Esther a 6-month internship at the CCC; she was called by Esther's uncle and is now letting Esther know that they will be delighted to have her.
Information about internship / institution CCC is a community center offering all kinds of services and advice to the people in the Ciderwood neighborhood, the focus is on childcare, educational classes (job interviews, computing skills, etc,) and health-related issues (keeping a healthy diet, low budget and nutrition, etc.).
They have a staff of 17 and are open six days a week from 7 am to 8 pm.
Nancy cannot offer Esther more than $85 a week to cover her costs for travel and meals.
Esther can start work on October 1 and finish on March 31.
Further information Esther should contact Nancy by mail (Nancy.Erlbaum@ccc-grandrapids.org) telling her about her decision.

Teil 2 Mediation

Results of a survey into eating and drinking habits of German children and teenagers in Bonn carried out by class 12BFS3 of Konrad-Adenauer-Berufskolleg, a local vocational college – summary of a newspaper article

The students of class 12BFS3 of Konrad-Adenauer-Berufskolleg analysed 450 questionnaires from different school types; the participants were between 7 and 25 years old.

These are the main results:
Most participants in the survey said that they hardly eat fast food and meat and regularly drink milk. For the age group of 14-17 the picture is quite different. One third of the teenagers eat fast food at least once a week and have ready-made meals and other convenience foods at least once a week, too. The majority admitted to not eating enough fish, vegetables and fruit. However, they consume more meat/sausages, chocolate and other sweets. Soft drinks and energy drinks are extremely popular with boys. The older the teenagers, the more soft drinks they consume.

About half of the boys and girls interviewed in the project said that they have fresh fruit at least once a day. However, the older the teenagers, the less attention they pay to healthy eating. Most people eat bread quite often. White bread and rolls are more popular than whole-grain bread.

All in all it can be said that the eating habits of teenagers get worse the older they are; girls tend to keep a more balanced diet than boys. In comparison to representative studies for the whole of Germany it can be said that not all details are identical, but on the whole there are many similarities to be found.

Teil 3 Rezeption (Leseverstehen)

Aspect	Information from the text
CCC	- CCC is a government-based neighborhood center - task: provide assistance and special advice for the people living in the area - focus lies on childcare, educational classes and health-related issues
Ciderwood area	- Ciderwood cannot be called a deprived neighborhood - increased demand for classes on educational, health-related issues - economic problems due to the closing of some car factories two years ago - unemployment rate 2% above the national average
Eating behaviour US teens	- evidence: teenagers from deprived neighborhoods are more prone to obesity - about 10 in 100 young American women suffer from eating disorders - since 1980, the number of overweight children in the USA has doubled - eating habits of teenagers: skipping meals, routine fast food consumption, frequent snacking and dieting - more than half of male teens and more than two-thirds of female teens do not eat breakfast on a regular basis

	- irregular schedules, convenience, work and social activities are the main reasons - fast food has replaced regular eating patterns - teens often diet because "thin is in" - more and more teenagers do not know how to keep a healthy diet, this is where the vicious circle of fast food and dieting starts
Advice given by CCC	- be active! (adults at least 30 minutes a day, children at least 60 minutes) - regular family meals - know what you eat - eat lean cuts, seafood and beans - avoid frying - eat low-fat or fat-free dairy products - variety of fruits, not too much juice - vary types of vegetables - half of grains consumed should be whole grains - make fast food an exception

Teil 4 Produktion (schriftlich)

Report on job-related work experience and activities in health and social care

As I am really interested in working in health and social care I have tried to improve my skills and expand my knowledge. Thus, I have so far attended a series of classes and have also done a couple of work placements.

At school (in year 9) we all had to do a student internship. I decided to work at the local hospital. They asked me if I would like to work in the children's ward and I agreed. I found the work very interesting, even though it was hard to see how little children had to suffer because they were ill.

Later, when I was 17, I worked as a youth coach and was involved in camping holidays for children. For three years running, we took about 30 children on a camping holiday to the Netherlands. The children were between 8 and 12 years old. Our tasks as youth coaches were cooking, supervision, games and sports activities. I found this experience very rewarding – not only the challenge of looking after the children, also the fun involved in organising the entire trip to make it worthwhile for the children.

I also attended a course at the local adult education centre, the Volkshochschule. They offered a class called "Keeping a healthy diet". It was a 2-week-class and took place in the summer holidays. I also took part in a first aid course.

When I started the two-year class at the vocational college we all had to do a 4-month internship again. Every day I worked at the local youth club. In the afternoons we organised homework supervision, games, sports and discussion rounds for the children and teenagers. I was given a lot of responsibility, which I liked a lot.

At college we did a class project on the eating behaviour of children and teenagers. We analysed about 450 questionnaires of participants who were between 7 and 25 years old. For me, the most striking result of this project was that the eating habits of teenagers get worse the older they are.

Teil 5 Produktion (eigene Stellungnahme)

Pro	Kontra
Verbot würde Fast Food Konsum deutlich einschränken.	Falsche Altersgruppe: Fast Food besonders beliebt bei älteren Jugendlichen.
Fast Food als „social event" würde wegfallen.	Erziehung zu verantwortungsbewusstem Essen funktioniert so nicht.
Eltern hätten mehr Kontrolle über das Essverhalten der Kinder.	Verbot setzt voraus, dass Eltern selbst kaum Fast Food konsumieren und ein Vorbild sind.
Kinder würden Geld sparen.	Verbote auch beim Essen können zu mehr heimlichem Fast Food Konsum führen.
Gesünderes Essen wäre die Folge.	Erziehung und Aufklärung statt Verbote
...	...

Practice Exam 2

Teil 1 Rezeption (Hörverstehen)

Hörtext, Track A 1.28

Active Silver Life currently owns and operates 11 state-of-the-art retirement villages throughout New Zealand, which makes the company New Zealand's leading provider of residential geriatric care. The company was founded in 1992 and has greatly contributed to a modern interpretation of eldercare in New Zealand.

Active Silver Life currently provides care for approximately 2,950 residents. Each of Active Silver Life's retirement villages offers amenities similar to a first-class holiday resort combined with a range of assisted living facilities. Assisted living can be defined as assistance with any kind of activities of daily living. This kind of assistance may include medical care or personal care services as provided by trained staff.

An Active Silver Life village offers its residents the choice of living independently in a home of their own or enjoying the comfort of living in serviced apartments. Residents can receive services such as regular household cleaning, laundry, meals, personal care and medical care. All homes have access to 24-hour emergency assistance and trained staff are on hand to assist residents. Of course all buildings and facilities are specially designed for use by disabled people. Bathrooms and kitchens are built with wheelchairs and walkers in mind; hallways and doors are extra-wide to accommodate wheelchairs.

Residents can use a variety of sports facilities such as a swimming pool, a gymnasium and a tennis court. Other facilities include a library, hairdressing salon, and a doctor's surgery as well as small shops and restaurants. Those residents who require 24-hour care in a safe, yet personal environment benefit from Active Silver Life's rest homes and hospitals, which you will also find in each retirement village.

A team of enthusiastic and trained staff look after the residents' well being, ensuring that their privacy and dignity is always respected.
Should you need further information about Active Silver Life, please write to
Active Silver Life House
302 Great Barrier Road
P O Box 3767
Wellington
New Zealand

or visit our website at www.activesilverlife.co.nz.

Aspect	Information from the radio programme
general information about Active Silver Life	- 11 state-of-the-art retirement villages throughout New Zealand - New Zealand's leading provider of residential geriatric care - founded in 1992 - has greatly contributed to a modern interpretation of eldercare in New Zealand - provides care for approximately 2,950 residents - address: Active Silver Life House, 302 Great Barrier Road, P O Box 3767, Wellington, New Zealand - www.activesilverlife.co.nz
Active Silver Life villages	- facilities: swimming pool, gymnasium, tennis court, library, hairdressing salon, doctor's surgery, shops, restaurants - rest homes and hospitals - residents live in a home of their own or in serviced apartments - services such as regular household cleaning, laundry, meals, personal care and medical care are available - access to 24-hour emergency assistance - buildings and facilities are designed for use by disabled people
Assisted living means …	- assistance with any kind of activities of daily living - may include medical care or personal care services provided by trained staff

Teil 2 Rezeption (Leseverstehen)

1. **fachliche und personale Anforderungen**

Active Silver Life sucht eine/n Bewerber/in, die/der wie folgt charakterisiert werden kann:
- erfahrene/r und qualifizierte/r Altenpfleger/in mit 5 Jahren Berufserfahrung
- engagiert, gutes Kommunikationsverhalten
- soll in der Lage und auch bereit sein, Verantwortung zu übernehmen
- Kenntnisse in den neuesten Entwicklungen auf dem Bereich der Altenpflege
- geduldig und ruhig
- teamfähig

2. **Stellenbeschreibung**

Active Silver Life sucht zwei Altenpfleger/innen für die Wohnanlagen in New Plymouth und Christchurch. Die Arbeitszeit beträgt 38 Stunden die Woche bei zwei Wochenenddiensten im Monat. Die Arbeitszeiten sind flexibel.

3. **Was bietet Active Silver Life?**

Active Silver Life bietet:
- ein motiviertes Mitarbeiterteam
- gute Unterstützungs- und Arbeitsstrukturen
- moderne Pflegeeinrichtungen, aktuelle Standards
- angemessene Bezahlung
- gute und andauernde Beziehungen zu Mitarbeitern und Patienten
- vielfache Möglichkeiten der beruflichen Weiterentwicklung

Teil 3 Mediation

German society is shrinking as well as aging.

Within the next 40 years, the German population will decrease to 74 million people. At the same time, every second man will be older than 51 and every second woman will be older than 53 years of age. The percentage of those over 65 will have doubled. There will also be significantly more citizens over 80 or even 100.
The majority of older people see a longer life as an increase in quality of life. On the whole they regard themselves as active and appreciate social contacts, their financial situation and life as such.
However, a longer life also means an increase in chronic diseases. Older people make increased use of the services of health and care systems.
This development means that nursing and care services have growing employment figures. With 4.4 m people already working in healthcare, these numbers are expected to continue to rise over the coming years and even decades. On the one hand the number of people who are ill and/or in need of care will increase significantly; on the other hand there is already a lack of qualified staff today. Unattractive working conditions, low pay and a strenuous job mean that the number of students who want to enter this profession is far too low.
Yet, many experts agree that one of the most decisive challenges an aging society has to meet is the supply of resources for health and care systems for the years to come.

Teil 4 Produktion (schriftlich)

Working as a registered nurse

Typical activities of a registered nurse for the elderly fall into several categories.

On the one hand there is the direct contact to the patient. This includes medical services as well as a more social and personal contact.
When talking about medical services, you need to mention standard routines such as skin care, change of bandages, injections, irrigations, various therapies and exercises. Of course medication and personal hygiene are very important daily activities, too. From time to time, being able to give first aid can save the patient's life.

On the other hand, the patients sometimes just need someone to help them with dressing or eating, someone who will just listen or encourage them to talk to the carer or other patients. Here, being part of the patient's social network is more important than being a medical specialist.

In addition there is the contact to family members and other staff. Team meetings are important; conversations with doctors and other staff are vital to exchange relevant information.

Of course, working as a registered nurse for the elderly means a lot of paperwork as well. There are reports that need to be written, and care procedures that have to be documented and also billed.

Finally, a lot of organisation and cooperation is necessary when events and parties for the elderly are planned and implemented.

Teil 5 Produktion (eigene Stellungnahme)

Pro (no further retirement villages)	**Kontra** (retirement villages are valuable institutions)
Families provide long-term social contacts.	They provide the structures and facilities families can never offer.
Family care does not cost as much as retirement villages.	Experienced and motivated staff who spend all their time on eldercare.
Many pensioners cannot afford retirement villages.	The elderly do not get the feeling that they are a burden on their families.
Retirement villages isolate the elderly, they are no longer part of society.	Highest degree of support and security.
Care and dedication given by family members mean more than qualified medical care.	Offer a new home for the elderly.
...	...

Practice Exam 3

Teil 1 Rezeption (Hörverstehen)

Hörtext, Track A 1.29

Good afternoon, Marie, this is Alison Hailey, from the Institute of Health Science at the University of Toronto.
Marie, about a month ago we talked about the conference on teenage addiction that is to be held in Germany. I promised to deliver a paper on the relationship between drug misuse and teenage pregnancy here in Toronto, Canada.

The reason I am phoning today is that I sent you my paper by mail the other week so that you could put it on your website. However, something must have gone wrong and I just noticed that I sent you the wrong document. It is on the same topic but it refers to a survey which is much older. I think the other survey was published in the late nineties. Of course I would prefer to use the updated results at your conference.
I tried to send you the correct version by mail yesterday, but for some reason my mail keeps coming back. I sent it to the email address I've always used which is m.wilbeul@GWSteglitz.de.

Could you please check if your email is working properly? If you have got a new email address, could you please send me a mail or give me a call. My email is a.hailey@healthscience.utoronto.ca.

Could you also please make sure that you exchange the documents on your website? I hope that not too many people have downloaded the wrong file ...

I hope that everything is fine in Germany and that you are on schedule with your preparations for the conference. I will be arriving a day early, which I believe is a Wednesday. I have a conference in Lisbon before your conference and I want to fly to Marseilles on the Saturday after the conference. I'm going to see my parents-in-law before I go back to Canada on Sunday night. Maybe we could get together if you have time.

I'll be in touch a week before the conference and see how you are getting on.
I look forward to hearing from you soon!
Bye for now.

Anrufer Alison Hailey
Institut/Einrichtung Institute of Health Science, Universität Toronto
Anlass Frau Hailey wird auf der Konferenz einen Vortrag zum Thema halten, sie hat den Vortrag auch schon per Mail nach Deutschland geschickt (für Homepage), hat aber aus Versehen älteres Dokument geschickt, will aktuelle Version mailen, Mail kommt aber zurück.
Weitere Informationen Kommt einen Tag eher, da sie von einer anderen Konferenz kommt, hat dann etwas Zeit am Samstag und hofft auf gemeinsame Zeit.
Zu veranlassende Schritte ihr die aktuelle Mailadresse schicken (a.hailey@healthscience.utoronto.ca) oder sie anrufen, dann die Dokumente auf der Homepage austauschen.

Teil 2 Mediation

According to experts, addictions count as the biggest and most costly problems of modern societies. In Europe more than 10% of all costs in the healthcare systems relate to the treatment of these illnesses.

The World Health Organisation WHO defines addiction as a pleasurable state of chronic or periodic intoxication. This intoxication is a consequence of taking natural or synthetic drugs.

Some critics argue that addiction is not only a matter of dependency on substances. With increasing internet saturation, for example, new forms of addictions which are based on behavioural patterns have developed.
Research into forms of addiction thus distinguishes between dependencies on substances and dependencies on certain behavioural patterns.
Legal and illegal substances may constitute a physical dependency. Alcohol, tobacco, coffee and tablets are to some extent legal, whereas the consumption of marijuana, crack, LSD, heroin and cannabis is against the law.
Satisfaction can also be gained through certain compulsive actions. These forms of addiction include computer and TV addiction, gambling and shopping addiction and eating or sex addiction.

Teil 3 Rezeption (Leseverstehen)

General trend
- we all are increasingly reliant on communication technology
- mobile phones are used as alarm clocks, watches, music players, cameras, calendars, for the weather forecast or as a navigation device
- mobile phones interfere with personal relationships, productivity at work, and traffic safety
- the cell phone is a device many people "can least go out without"

Teenagers and mobile phone use
- several hours a day, even at night

Excessive use and its consequences
- teenagers have a generally more careless lifestyle
- they consume more stimulating beverages
- they have difficulty in falling asleep and suffer from disrupted sleep
- they are more susceptible to stress and fatigue

Symptoms of mobile phone addiction
- neglecting the obligations of important activities (e.g. job or studies)
- showing irrational reactions without a phone
- spending more and more time talking on a cell phone
- getting higher mobile phone bills that cause financial distress
- having problems at school and work from constant cell phone use
- having interpersonal problems from constant cell phone use
- taking unnecessary risks such as using a cell phone while driving

Tips to prevent mobile phone addiction
- phone use only at specific times during the day
- prepaid cards
- activities and hobbies without phones (sports)

Teil 4 Produktion (schriftlich)

The diagram shows the number of children and teenagers who had to be treated in German hospitals because of alcohol poisoning. The figures are given for the years 2000 and 2008. When looking at the development for male children and teenagers aged between 10 and 19, it must be said that the number of those who had to be treated in hospital nearly tripled from 6,000 in 2000 to 16,000 in 2008. The girls showed a dramatic increase as well, here the number more than doubled from just under 4,000 cases to nearly 10,000. So for both boys and girls the number of those who suffered from alcohol poisoning because of binge drinking exploded. When looking at the difference between male and female drinkers it can be said that the number of boys who consume dangerous amounts of alcohol are considerably higher for both years.

Teil 5 Produktion (eigene Stellungnahme)

Pro (law for the protection of the youth still makes sense)	**Kontra** (law for the protection of the youth does not make sense any more)
Taking drugs remains dangerous, therefore teenagers need to be protected.	These laws are old-fashioned because there are more substances and addictions than most state representatives know about.
Taking drugs must continue to be regarded as negative and bad; making it illegal helps.	It is impossible to adjust the legal system to ever new forms of addiction.
Drug trafficking is not that rewarding if not many teenagers take illegal drugs.	Laws need to be changed to include other dangers of addiction as well (Internet, TV).
If there is no law protecting children and teenagers, there will be severe consequences for their health if they legally consume substances.	Parents are responsible for their children, not the state; a law cannot replace parents.
Even if the state cannot protect children and teenagers against all possible harm, there still need to be laws to clearly say that they are children and that they are protected as children.	Making drugs illegal turns those who take drugs into criminals.
…	…

social & health EXPERT
Soziales & Gesundheit
Lösungsheft zum Workbook

Autoren: Ephrem Wellenbrock, Dorsten; David Christie, Oxford

Berater: Hans-Henning Jasper, Monika Schumacher

1. Auflage 1 5 4 3 2 1 | 14 13 12 11 10

Alle Drucke dieser Auflage sind unverändert und können im Unterricht nebeneinander verwendet werden.
Die letzte Zahl bezeichnet das Jahr des Druckes.

Projektleitung: Matthias Rupp
Redaktion: Astrid Keller
Herstellung: Angelika Lindner

Gestaltung: B2 Büro für Gestaltung, Andreas Staiger, Stuttgart
Umschlaggestaltung: B2 Büro für Gestaltung, Andreas Staiger, Stuttgart
Satz: B2 Büro für Gestaltung, Andreas Staiger, Susanne Kunz, Stuttgart
Reproduktion: Meyle + Müller Medien-Management, Pforzheim
Druck: Mediahaus Biering GmbH, München

Printed in Germany
ISBN 978-3-12-800118-0

social & health EXPERT

Soziales & Gesundheit

Lösungsheft zum Workbook

Dieses Lösungsheft ist Bestandteil von:

ISBN 978-3-12-**800118**-0